SHRI RAMA CHANDRA

THE IDEAL KING

CENTRAL HINDU COLLEGE LECTURES. II.

SHRI RAMA CHANDRA

THE IDEAL KING

SOME LESSONS FROM THE RAMAYANA

FOR THE USE OF HINDU STUDENTS IN THE SCHOOLS OF INDIA

by

ANNIE BESANT, F. T. S.

FROM NOTES OF LECTURES ORIGINALLY DELIVERED

AT THE CENTRAL HINDU COLLEGE, BENARES.

GYAN

Published by

GYAN

Gyan Publishing House
5, Ansari Road
Daryaganj, New Delhi-110002
Phone: 011-47034999, 9811692060
E-mail: books@gyanbooks.com

Distribution Network
gyanbooks.com
India, USA, Canada, UK, Australia, France

ISBN : 978-81-212-6162-3 (PB)
First Published, 1901

2nd Impression 2021

Printed at: Gyan Press, Delhi.

Shri Rama Chandra
Author: Annie Besant

CENTRAL HINDU COLLEGE LECTURES. II.

SHRÎ RÂMA CHANDRA

THE IDEAL KING.

SOME LESSONS FROM THE RÂMÂYANA

FOR THE USE OF HINDU STUDENTS IN
THE SCHOOLS OF INDIA

BY

ANNIE BESANT, F. T. S.

FROM NOTES OF LECTURES ORIGINALLY DELIVERED

AT THE CENTRAL HINDU COLLEGE, BENARES.

1901.

CONTENTS.

SHRÎ RÂMA CHANDRA,

THE IDEAL KING.

CHAPTER I.

INTRODUCTION.

Two years ago we were studying together "one of the greatest books in the world," the *Mahâbhârata*. Now we are going to study the second great epic poem of India, the *Râmâyana*. These two books stand out from the rest of Indian literature in a very marked way. The *Vedas*, the *Institutes of Manu*, are the great authorities for the learned, and only through the learned for the mass of the people. But the *Mahâbhârata* and the *Râmâyana* are wrought into the very life of every Indian—man, woman and child. Mothers tell their stories to their children, teachers to their pupils, the old to the young. Every child grows up knowing the heroes of these poems as familiar friends, having been moved to tears and laughter from earliest days by these loved names.

Despite the influence wielded by these two books, however, their moulding power on life is not as great as once it was. If we could bring back their influence on character, we should indeed lift our India upwards. They hold up to us ideals of conduct, virtues acted out on life's stage as practical examples for old and young alike, for husbands and wives, parents and children, brothers and sisters, friends and enemies. This is even more true of the *Râmâyana* than of the *Mahâbhârata*. For in the vast story told in the *Mahâbhârata*, we have the picture of an age when life was very complex and relations very tangled—it is a modern drama. Good and evil are everywhere intermingled in the characters drawn for us, and scarcely one—save the blameless Bhîshma—shows us an ideally perfect man. The great Avatâra, of course, stands apart as superhuman. It is a book for men who have developed intellect and judgment, and who can trace the connection between sin and sorrow.

In the *Râmâyana* we move in a different atmosphere, and breathe an air of heroic simplicity. The characters are sharply cut—one is to followed, another is to be shunned. Good is good, evil is evil. Black is black, white is white, and there are no greys. Great types stand forth as ideals of right and wrong. The young can feel their inspiring beauty or their repellent ugliness. Can a Hindu wife have fairer and sweeter exemplar than the gracious Sîtâ? Can a Hindu prince shape himself on more regal lines than those of Râmachandra? Can a Hindu brother find a nobler type of fraternal devotion than Lakshmana? Why, the very names carry a thrill through every Hindu heart. All the melody of their lives sounds sweetly out when the key-note of their names is struck.

Nor should we forget that we owe to these great poems most of what is known publicly of ancient India. Therein we see how the national, social and family life was carried on, the ways of living, the joys and sorrows, the education of the young, the ideas of the populace. To think of ancient India, with all that we have learned from these books blotted out, would be to gaze at a blurred canvas instead of a living picture.

The *Râmâyana*, then, is to be the subject of our study, a study that will, I hope, be practically profitable. May we see, as we study character after character, the lessons each is meant to teach, and their value to us in modern India.

Let us glance first at the circumstances which surrounded the composition of the original *Râmâyana*. We read that the great sage Vâlmiki met another great sage, Nârada, and asked if there was on earth a perfect man, knowing duty, grateful and truthful, with heart and passions subdued, and intelligence evolved. To him answered Nârada, that such a one there was, a prince of the great line of Ikshvâku, named Râma. Patient, self-controlled and learned was he, of noble beauty and of manly strength, heroic in war and gentle in peace, beloved by all around him. Then Nârada briefly outlined his history, and told how he was then ruling his kingdom with justice and kindness, being as a father to his happy subjects.

Nârada described the state of Râmachandra's kingdom in glowing terms, telling how disease and famine did not touch it, nor fire nor flood. Fathers did not lose their sons, nor wives their husbands. Corn and wealth were everywhere, and no man feared hunger or theft. (Vâlakâṇḍam § i.) Such is the happy story of a nation where prince and people join together in righteous life and devotion to the comnon good. Material prosperity follows on the heels of spiritual life. Material welfare is the blessing bestowed by the Gods on the nation that lives nobly, wherein each performs his Dharma. If a nation falls in the scale of nations, the fault lies in itself; and if it would rise again, it must lay a fòundation of righteous living, and on that prosperity can be builded and on no other. The future of India lies with you, her younger sons, and if you grow up into a noble manhood, your country will grow up with you, and thus will rise among the peoples of the world.

His mind filled with this glowing picture of an ideal king, Vâlmiki went on his way, and as he walked through the forest he marked with pleasure the happy sights and sounds around him, the playful animals, the merry birds. And as he was watching a pair of Kraunchas sporting with each other, a fowler shot one of the harmless birds, and the hen-bird fluttered round her dying mate, uttering piercing cries. Then Vâlmiki, pitiful as are all good men, and knowing that cruelty brings misery in its track, cried out that he who had thus slain the happy bird should never attain prosperity. The words fell into the form of a shloka, musical and sonorous, and Brahmâ, appearing to the sage, bade him tell the story of Râma in that melodious measure, declaring that as long as mountain and sea existed, so long should his poem spread among men. Thus from a heart of love and pity was born the melody of the *Râmâyana*, and wherever it is chanted love and pity still find birth. (§ ii.)

But Vâlmiki needed more than the metre of his

poem; he needed its materials. So he sat him down and engaged in meditation on the subject, till the inner vision opened, and he saw "before him Râma and Lakshmana and Sîtâ, and Dasharatha together with his wives in his kingdom, laughing and talking and acting, and bearing themselves as in real life." (§ iii.) Thus he watched the history unroll itself before him, a living picture, true in every detail; for no event occurs that does not leave an imperishable record in that subtle âkâsha which surrounds and interpenetrates all.

There are two ways of gaining knowledge. One the way of study, by which we may learn what other people know and have written down for the instruction of those who know not. The second way is by developing within ourselves the nature which is knowledge, the nature which can reproduce within itself all to which it turns its attention, as the eye reflects the object at which it looks. Now the second way is the better, though by far the more difficult. We must prepare ourselves for it by treading the first. We must develop and train our intelligence by learning that which is written by men wiser than ourselves: then later in life, we may pass onward into the second path, and evolve the inner nature till it can see and know, and need seek no aid from books.

Thus did Vâlmiki see the story and invent the metre for its telling, and then he told it in twenty-four thousand shlokas, which have been grouped into five hundred chapters, and these again into seven Kâṇḍas, or Sections.

But still the poem needed means to reach the public ear in an age when knowledge passed from mouth to ear instead of from hand to eye. And Vâlmiki pondered: "Who shall sing this poem in assemblies?" While he thus pondered, two young ascetics came in and touched his feet; and these were the brothers Kusa and Lava, who were sons of Râma, though they knew it not—how and why this strange thing happened we shall learn hereafter. Finding that these youths were gifted with sweet voices and were skilled in music, he taught to them his wondrous poem, and going forth they sang it "in the assemblies of ascetics and of Brâhmaṇas and of all good men." And thus singing, they came to Ayodhya, where Râma ruled in royal splendour, and were seen of Him as they walked along a street. Then Râma's heart was drawn to the handsome modest youths, and He sent for them and bade them sing in presence of Himself and of His court. And thus they sang of Râma's birth and life, of His sorrows and His troubles, of Sîtâ and Lakshmana and Bharata and all the rest, in the very ears of the heroes of the story. And all men wondered as they listened to the wondrous tale, and marked the singers who bore the signs of royal birth upon them, though seeming but as two young ascetics in outward garb and mien.

Before we listen to their song, we must consider the time at which it was given, and the significance of the coming of Shrî Râma.

The period of the world's history at which Râmachandra lived was the closing of the Treta Yuga. The history of the world—and indeed of any separate nation—is divided into four great periods, or Yugas, named respectively the Sattya, the Treta, the Dvâpara, the Kali. Shrî Râma ruled during the last part of the Treta Yuga, and when He passed away from earth the Dvâpara Yuga began. That Yuga, again, was closed by the coming of Shrî Kriṣhṇa, and with His death was opened the Kali Yuga.

And what was Shrî Râma? Not simply a great warrior, a mighty king. He was an Avatâra, a divine incarnation, and a divine incarnation of a special kind. All men are divine incarnations. In the heart of every man the supreme Self abides. It is that Self who presses us onward and upward, who continues a never-failing pressure to which we are indeed blessed if we yield. But when we speak of an Avatâra, we mean more than this. An Avatâra (from "tṛi," pass over, and "ava," a prefix implying descent) is a special incarnation, a human form being taken in which the Divinity veils Himself and through which shines forth His glory. Not in germ, in "divine fragments," as in us, but in the full radiance of Deity, God reveals Himself in man to man.

For such coming there is always special reason, and one reason is the strengthening of the forces that work for good and the weakening of those that work for evil. This may be said to be the most general reason :

यदा यदाहिधर्मस्य ग्लानिर्भवति भारत ।
अभयुत्थानमधर्मस्य तदात्मानं सृजाम्यहम् ॥
परित्राणाय साधूनां विनाशायच दुष्कृताम् ।
धर्मसंस्थापनार्थाय संभवामि युगेयुगे ॥

"When Dharma decays, when Adharma is exalted, O Bhârata, then I myself come forth. For the protection of the good, for the destruction of the evil, for the firm establishment of Dharma, I am born from age to age." (*Bhagavad-gîta*, IV. 7, 8.)

Another question arises in connection with the Avatâras in Their aspect as Destroyers of evil. The world-process is carried on by means of opposing forces. The world is unfolding all the powers of the inner life breathed into it by Îshvara. As a seed is placed in the ground and grows into a plant bearing flowers and, within them, fruits, so is it with the world; a seed of divine life is planted in matter, and grows into a world, bearing humanity as its flower, a flower that yields the fruit of divinity. For we also are Gods, but Gods in the making.

In order that this evolution may take place, two things are necessary—two forces that apparently work the one against the other. One pushes on evolution and that is seen as helping it. The other pushes against evolution, and that is seen as hindering it. But the appearance deludes us. The force that pushes against evolution is as necessary for it as the one which pushes it onwards. Think of a wheel—the wheel of a bicycle, if you like. You can turn the wheel round very quickly in the air, but then the bicycle does not go on; only when you place the wheel on the ground, which offers resistance to it, can it go on. Motion is only possible where there is resistance. You can only leap by having firm ground to stand on which resists the pressure of your feet. This resistance which makes possible the forward movement of the world is called "evil." But you must understand clearly that it only helps you when you push against it. If you were to lie down on the ground instead of pushing your feet hard against it, you would not rise into the air. And if you yield to evil instead of resisting it, it will not draw forth your strength. Evil is used rightly when we strive against it, for then the efforts call out our divine nature. Evil is God's servant as much as good, but serves Him in a different way.

In your athletic exercises you exert yourselves, and thereby grow strong. You use dumb-bells and Indian clubs, and by exerting your muscles against their weight, you make your muscles grow. When you race, and play football and cricket, you are exerting your strength to overcome obstacles, and your strength grows. If you are lazy and slothful, you cannot become strong; only exercise increases strength. So evil calls on the soul to exert itself and conquer it. Remember that when you yield to evil, it pushes you back; when you strive against it, it gives you the resistance that enables you to go forward.

When these forces of resistance are growing too strong by men's yielding to them, so that they threaten to retard evolution, then an Avatâra comes to restore the due proportion, and the forces of evil are drawn together, usually culminating in a single individual, and this individual appears as the opponent of the Avatâra. Râvana plays this part in the *Râmâyana*. Râmachandra stands for the Good, Râvana for the Evil, and they struggle together, and Râmachandra triumphs. After the triumph of the Good, the Evil shows that it also has its root in Îshvara, for Râvana, slain by Râma, ascends to Viṣhṇu's heaven.

But there are other reasons also for the coming of an Avatâra. Sometimes He is also a Teacher, as in the case of Shrî Kriṣhṇa, whose divine "Song" is still the world's wonder. Sometimes He is also an Example; and as an example for men of the world—not for the recluse, the ascetic, the sannyâsi, but for the son, the husband, the brother, the ruler, the warrior, the man who would lead a spiritual life in the world—Râmachandra stands supreme, the ideal man in every relation of life. Ideal king and warrior, the beauty of his character also shines out in all His domestic relations, in those ties which bind the home, and therefore society, together. Among all the great ones who stand out in Indian literature, there is none whose life serves as a more noble and practical model than that of Him who came down to show what a man might be, and to illumine human relations with divine light.

Especially was it Shrî Râma's mission to shew

forth the ideal Kshattriya. For the Kshattriya caste had abused its strength and right of rule, and, like many strong men, had become tyrannous. It had used its power for oppression instead of for protection, for self instead of for others. The strong man's duty is to defend the weak, never to tyrannise over him. So is it the strong boy's duty to protect the little boys, and to see that they are not unfairly used. A big boy who strikes a little boy is a coward, and is looked down upon by brave boys.

Now the Kshattriya caste had been cut down to its very roots by Parashurâma, as a punishment for its abuse of power. He slew them, that they might learn that those who used strength to oppress and slay would be slain by a power greater than their own. When that stern lesson had been taught by Râma of the Axe, then Râmachandra came to serve as model for the ideal Kshattriya.

We shall study this ideal in detail, but I may say of it in this introductory lecture that it is one which sorely needs revival in modern India. There come out in it very strongly what are called the manly virtues which are needed to make a nation great; among these are courage, strength, patience, endurance, self-respect, readiness to stand up in defence of right and against wrong, much vital energy and nervous force. These manly virtues were very conspicuous in Indian heroes in the past, but are lamentably deficient in the India of to-day. No nation can be great which lets slip out of its character these strong and virile virtues, and we must re-build them in India's sons.

Do not think that these virtues must be accompanied by aggressive insolence or roughness, though they are too often thus attended. There was nothing of insolence or roughness in Râmachandra. He was very gentle and compassionate, very courteous and well-mannered, showing a tender reverence to his parents, deference to the aged and the learned. You must seek to build into your characters courage and self-respect along with sweetness and courtesy: then you will be ideals of manliness, strong and gentle.

Try not to be afraid of those above you in age or in social position. A boy should not be afraid of his father or of his teacher, but while he should treat them with respect, he should have frank confidence in their good-will. Be frank, brave, honest and courteous, and you will be beloved and trusted by your superiors. No brave man likes others to cringe to him, and he treats manliness with respect.

Turning now to the story, we learn something

about the place in which Râmachandra was to be born. It was in the city of Ayodhya, the capital of the country of Koshala, the city the very name of which means the unconquerable. In this city a king descended from the great Ikshvâku was ruling; the land was watered by the pleasant river Sarayu, and was prosperous and wealthy. A very attractive description of this city is given, and the details shew us the high state of civilisation that had been reached. The roads were broad, and were kept well-watered and strewn with blossoms. There were shops filled with goods of all descriptions, and artisans and merchants of all kinds. There were public buildings such as theatres, and splendid palaces and pleasure-grounds. The soldiers there were chosen for their skill in wielding weapons combined with propriety in their use; they would "slaughter infuriated lions and tigers and boars roaming in the forest," but "would not pierce with arrows persons lorn, or abandoned, or hiding, or fugitive." They guarded the peaceful against attack whether from man or beast, but wrought no harm on helpless folk. And Brâhmaṇas too were there, pious, virtuous and learned, "ever abiding by truth, high-souled, and resembling mighty ascetics." (§ v.)

Such a population was naturally prosperous and

well-to-do, and it is remarked that each was "contented with his possessions," and that there were no poor and none who were unlettered.

Would that we could say the same of modern India, but now-a-days only the few are educated, while the vast majority are left in ignorance. Contentment, also, is not a very widespread virtue, though one most productive of happiness. Contentment does not depend on position, nor on wealth, but on mind. It is an attitude of the mind, not a result of circumstances. Many a poor man is contented with the little he has, while many a rich man is discontented with his abundance. The mind is the root alike of content and of discontent.

All the citizens, it is said further, were of good character, pure and clean in mind and body, and hence it was that "no man and no woman was seen devoid of grace or beauty," for physical beauty and grace are attendants on pure character and refined ways of life. (§ vi.)

Another cause of happiness for the people was the goodness and diligence of their king, Dasharatha, and the wisdom with which he chose his counsellors. These are described as being devoted to their monarch, ever intent on his good, learned and modest, conversant with policy, self-controlled, energetic, gentle in speech, and "never committing themselves to a lie from anger or interest or desire." With such a monarch and such counsellors, well might the people be happy. (§ vii.)

But there was a shadow in all this brightness: the king was childless, and he was very old. King and people alike longed to see an heir to the throne, and the king therefore betook himself to prayer and sacrifice. (§ viii.) A learned and famous sage, Ṛishyashṛinga, was chosen as the leader of the sacrificial ceremony, the horse sacrifice (§ ix-xiii.), and after all preparations had been duly made, the king and his wives were initiated for the performance of the rites. (§ xiii.) It is noteworthy that no Brâhmaṇa was allowed to officiate who "was not versed in the Vedas and Vedângas, or that did not observe vows, or that was not profoundly learned, nor did any assist at the sacrifice that did not argue ably." The illiterate or ignorant Brâhmaṇa was regarded as no Brâhmaṇa in those happier times. Then was the dictum of Manu no idle word: "As an elephant made of wood, as an antelope made of leather, such is an unlearned Brâhmaṇa: these three have nothing but the names." (ii. 157.) No ceremony is rightly done where the officiating priest is ignorant; knowledge, purity, truthfulness—where these are absent, the chant of the priest cannot reach the Gods. Only where the sacrifice is rightly performed, will the great Ones deign to be present.

It is interesting to note that at this great public ceremony, attended by crowds of Brâhmaṇas, kings, nobles and warriors, the celebrant was a woman—Kaushalyâ, the eldest wife of king Dasharatha. Among the many precious things which ancient India possessed and which modern India has lost, is the position held by women. The restoration of the old position is a necessary condition of the revival of national greatness, for the influence of the mother weighs greatly in the development of the son. (§ xiv.)

After the completion of the horse-sacrifice, that for conferring a son was performed, and at this the Gods prayed to Brahmâ that He would devise some means for destroying Râvana, the great Râkshasa, who, by virtue of a boon conferred on him by Brahmâ Himself, was harassing the three worlds. "The sun does not burn him, nor does the wind blow on him; and at sight of him the one engarlanded with billows, the Ocean, dares not stir." By men alone, answered Brahmâ, could Râvana be slain, for He had given him immunity from death at the hand of other beings; Râvana, in his pride, did not include men among his possible assailants, hence only by men could he be slain.

Then Vishṇu appeared, bearing the conch, the discus and the mace, objects that are always placed in the hands of the upholder of the worlds. Now these objects are not meaningless, but each is a symbol of a divine power. The conch symbolises sound, the creative power which shapes matter into forms. The chakram, or discus, is the symbol of destruction, the whirling vibratory forces that shatter the worlds. The mace is the rod of power, the sign of the protecting and supporting forces that preserve the universe. You may see these symbols in the temples in connection with Viṣhṇu, and you should know their meanings.

Viṣhṇu, thus appearing, promised the Gods that He would take birth as man and would slay Râvana, and that He would become the four sons that should be born to king Dasharatha. (§ xv.)

As Viṣhṇu vanished, there arose out of the sacrificial fire a radiant being, bearing a golden vessel filled with celestial Pâyasa, which, as the messenger of Prajâpati, the Lord of offspring, he gave to the king for his three wives. This the king joyfully divided among them, and they became mothers. (§ xvi.)

But ere the children were born, preparation was made for the struggle that lay before them. The

Gods created great hosts of creatures of many forms, half divine, half brute, bears and monkeys of super-physical powers, able to change their shapes at will—strange astral creatures, assuming animal forms. Indra created Vâli, and Aditya Sugriva—monkey chiefs that we shall meet hereafter. And Visvakarman, the celestial architect, produced Nala, who was to build the bridge over the ocean. And Vâyu called into being the famous Hanumân, for whose sake all monkeys range at will all Indian temples and gardens even to the present day. (§ xvii.)

Thus was all made ready for the coming of Shri Râma.

CHAPTER II.

YOUTH AND MARRIAGE.

King Dasharatha, it is written, dwelt in Ayodhya "happily, expecting sons," and the whole world was waiting with him, for Vishṇu was coming in human form to His earth. All-pervading, all-supporting, He was to fill with His life these coming children, that they might manifest Him in the world for the world's helping.

The seasons rolled on in due order, and when the Sun was in Aries, the Moon in Capricornus, Saturn in Libra, Jupiter in Cancer aud Venus in Pisces, there was born of Kaushalyâ a splendid boy, strong and comely, "the one half of Vishṇu." After he was born, Kaikeyî gave birth to a son, and Sumitrâ also to twin-sons, and these were the four brothers, who were the four forms of one life, Righteousness, and Truth, and Fidelity and Heroism incarnate. And they were named with all due forms by Vasishṭha, and the son of Kaushalyâ was named Râma, and the son of Kaikeyî Bharata while the two sons of Sumitrâ were called Lakshmaṇa and Shatrughna.

Great were the rejoicings in Ayodhya, and players and dancers filled the streets, while the king fed all the multitude and gave rich gifts to Brâhmaṇas. And heavenly musicians and dancers, the sweetly playing Gandharvas and sportive Apsarâs, filled the air with joyous strains and merry laughter, for all were glad, both Gods and men, that Shrì Râma and His brothers were born into the world.

This common rejoicing of the inhabitants of earth and heaven and the middle plane—of the three worlds—is a marked feature in the coming of very great Ones. We read of it in the various Scriptures of the religions of the world. The Buddha was hymned by Devas when born of Mâyâ, as was Jesus by Angels when born of Mary. The higher worlds are not far off, but are round us all the time, and sometimes the veils of matter are rent asunder and their habitants mingle in a common joy.

As the children grew up, they were carefully educated, so that in their manhood they might serve their country well. And we may learn from the education given to them what was the training which, in ancient India, was thought suitable as a preparation for an active life in the world For these boys were not to be recluses and ascetics, but men of the world, with a part to play therein, and we may learn from the studies assigned to them what was then deemed necessary to prepare a lad for active life. First and foremost were placed religion and morality; they became versed in the Vedas, and were taught to be ever intent on the welfare of others. Then they were thoroughly instructed in the various branches of knowledge, and were trained in arms, riding, and the management of cars. Thus the four parts of a complete education, spiritual, moral, intellectual, and physical, were all duly attended to, and the lads grew towards manhood, the beloved of all and the joy of their father's heart.

We find stress laid in the old books on the physical side of education, the training of the body, a thing much neglected in modern India. A boy has a body as well as a mind, and the body should be healthy, strong and well developed, so that he may have a useful instrument for all good work. Where the body is weak, the work of the mind is injured. True, the body is to be subordinate, your servant and under your control. Over and over again we read that the brothers controlled their senses, were masters of their bodies. But just as in choosing a horse, you do not choose a weak, diseased creature, but look for strong muscles, high spirit and endurance, and expect the animal to be subject to your control: so you should try to make your bodies strong, healthy and vigorous, full of energy, full of power, full of life, but under the control of the higher nature, trained to serve all good and great purposes under the direction of the will, subordinate to the divine purpose, ready to serve God and man with energy and devotion.

The education given in this College is founded on this ancient model, this fourfold training. Instruction in the Hindu religion is placed in the forefront, because we know that education without religion is destructive of the highest interests of the nation, and renders it impossible that the Indian people shall become a great nation. Moral and intellectual education is also given, and we lay stress on the training of the body, on games and manly exercises. May such education give to India citizens worthy of her past!

Shrî Râma was the pride and delight of His father, even above His brothers, for He shone above them, pre-eminent in excellence. The brothers themselves went in pairs—Râma and Lakshmaṇa, Bharata and Shatrughna. Lakshmaṇa, we read, "was like unto another life of Râma......in everything attentive to Râma's wishes, even to the neglect of his own person." And he "did not even sleep without Râma's company, nor partake of any dainty food unless Râma shared it with him. And when Râma went out hunting on horse-back, Lakshmaṇa went at his back, bow in hand, protecting Him. And that younger brother of Lakshmaṇa, Shatrughna, became ever dearer to Bharata than life itself."

One detail of Râmachandra's life we learn outside the *Râmâyaṇa*. When His regular education was completed and the pomp of royal state and the joy of young manhood lay before Him, a great weariness came upon Him and all savour departed from life. He turned listlessly away from all interest and all pleasure, gentle, sweet and submissive ever, but utterly indifferent to everything, turning away from the fair earth His tired eyes. In vain His father, His brothers, sought to cheer Him, in vain were pleasures spread before Him, in vain did teachers and friends strive to rouse Him. He sat alone, with eyes down-dropped and drooping head—for Vairâgya was upon Him, the distaste for the passing, for the unreal, the sick longing for the Eternal, the Reality, the Truth. How He was lifted thereout into the clear air of changeless Wisdom by the great sage, Vasiṣhṭha, you may read when you are older in that storehouse of occult knowledge, the *Yoga Vâsiṣhṭha.*

Enough here to say that He was lifted out of it, and took up His life in the world again with all its duties, with free spirit and open vision, as son instead of slave. For He had learned the Science of Peace, the Science of the Self, that Science which, once understood in its fulness, shows all earthly things indeed as empty without satisfying power, but also gives them their true place as helpers in the evolution of man. One who has thus learned is more diligent in work than the man of the world, though utterly indifferent to work's objects for himself, and rejoicing only in the Self.

When he was thus made ready, the call to public duty sounded in the air.

One day as king Dasharatha sat among his counsellors, discussing the question of Râma's marriage, the great ascetic Vishvâmitra knocked at his gate, and bade the warders tell the king that he had come. We shall hear his story presently, when it is told to Shrî Râma.

With joy king Dasharatha hurried out to meet his revered guest, and offered him the Arghya in due form, and brought him into his palace. Then he eagerly asked what service he could do him to shew his devotion; "What is nearest thy heart? What shall I do for thee? I will in everything do thy will; thou art my God." Thus without reserve he pledged himself, unthinking. (§. xviii.)

Then answered Vishvâmitra smiling: " Mayst thou be as firm in promise as thou art ready in speech." And he told him how he was celebrating a sacrifice and was disturbed by two Râkshasas, Mârîcha and Suvâhu, who poured blood and flesh on the altar, polluting it, and thus hindered the completion of the ceremony. " Give me then, Râma thy first-born, this heroic youth, for he shall be able to destroy them, and he alone can do it. For ten nights only need he be there, and all will be well. He is of age and full of valour. Grant me then Râma, O mighty king!"

When this most unexpected demand fell on his ears, king Dasharatha was so taken aback that for awhile he sat speechless. [§ xix.] Send Râma to engage in battle so perilous with foes so fierce, his Râma, his first-born, still a youth—nay, that he could not do. Hastily, brokenly, his words poured forth. He would go himself; he would take his army; but Râma was dearest to him of all his sons, all born to him in his extreme age; he could not part from Râma. And who were these Râkshasas, and by whom supported? Then sounded out on Râma's listening ears the name of His great foe: Râvaṇa, son of Vishravan, mightiest of all

Râkshasas, conqueror of the three worlds, not deigning himself to mar the sacrifice, sent Mârîcha and Suvâhu as his agents. "Against Râvaṇa," cried the king, "I cannot fight. None may stand against him in battle, for none may face him and live. And Râma! this my son is a boy though beautiful and strong as an immortal. I will not part with my son." [§ xx].

Then Vishvâmitra answered sternly: "Having first promised, thou dost now renounce thy promise. Unworthy is this of Raghu's descendant, evil is this for thy house. Behold, I go hence to my place. O king, false in promise, mayst thou find happiness among thy friends."

The grave displeasure of Vishvâmitra the mighty alarmed the sages and the worlds, for it is ill done when the Great Ones are refused aught they ask. For they ask not for themselves, but for the welfare of the worlds, and all they ask is good. Thereupon Vasiṣhṭha interfered, reminding the king that a pledged word might not be broken, and that he must therefore give Râma to Vishvâmitra, but consoling him by telling him that Vishvâmitra could defend his own sacrifice were it necessary, and only asked for Râma for Râma's own good. [§ xxi.]

Then Dasharatha gave Râma into the hands of Vishvâmitra, and the great ascetic set forth, followed by Râma and Lakshmaṇa, and they journeyed for several days, the youths serving Vishvâmitra dutifully, as befitted them, performing their daily Sandhyâ, and being delighted with the conversation of the sage. [§§ xxii. xxiii.]

During the journey Râma slew Târakâ, the fierce Râkshasî, the mother of Mârîcha [§§ xxiv—xxvi.], and received from Vishvâmitra many celestial weapons. [§§ xxvii. xxviii.] When they arrived at the hermitage of the ascetic, they heard its history from his lips: how it had been the hermitage of Vâmana the wondrous Dwarf; here was the field of battle where Râma was to meet his foes. [§ xxix.] As the sacrifice began the Râkshasas appeared, and Mârîcha was whirled out of sight by a shaft, striking him full on the chest, and dropped senseless into the ocean; Suvâhu also fell to the ground before the youthful warrior, and the inferior Râkshasas were slain and the sacrifice completed. [§ xxx.] But Mârîcha was to work woe to Râma in later days.

On the following day the ascetics present spoke of a wonderful bow, possessed by king Janaka of Mithilâ, and as that king was offering a great sacrifice, they decided to go thither. Forth they all fared together, and as they rested from time to time the brothers heard many a story connected with the scenes amid which they wandered and the hermitages in which they slept. They heard of Gangâ's descent on the head of Mahâdeva, of king Sagara and his sons, of the churning of the ocean, and of the drinking of the poison by Shiva. As they approached Mithilâ, they came to an empty hermitage, once the home of Gautama, and learned how Gautama's wife, Ahalyâ, was dwelling there invisible, as penalty for crime committed, awaiting the coming of Râma, who should restore her to the visible world. And on His coming she appeared again in body, and was re-united to her lord. After this, the ascetics and the brothers came to Mithilâ, where they were welcomed by king Janaka, to whom Vishvâmitra related all their adventures, and the desire of Râma to see the wondrous bow. [§§ xxxi—l.]

Then Satânanda, the son of Gautama, delighted to hear of the re-union of his father and mother, related to Râma the story of Vishvâmitra, a most instructive story. For it tells how a human soul took his own evolution in hand and forced himself onward to the desired goal. Vishvâmitra was born of royal blood and came duly to the throne in succession to Gâdhi, his father. He ruled for long, and once, when out with his army, he came to the hermitage of Vasiṣhṭha and was welcomed by him graciously. After pleasant converse, Vasiṣhṭha begged the king to accept his hospitality, he and his army with him, but the king wished to depart, saying courteously that Vasiṣhṭha's words of kindness had already fulfilled all hospitable rites. The sage, however, pressed him to remain, and by his wondrous cow, Savalâ, was produced all that was necessary for the feeding of the guests. Then king Vishvâmitra's heart was entered by envy and he offered large gifts in exchange for the cow, but Vasiṣhṭha would not part with his treasured animal. Whereupon the king, forgetful of all duty in his greed for the cow, took her away by force, but she escaped and returned to her owner, and "by her lowing" beings were produced that began to slay the armies of the king, till they were destroyed. Then the hundred sons of Vishvâmitra rushed on Vasiṣhṭha, and were consumed by him in a moment. The king, confounded, went away and began practising austerities, to war on Vasiṣhṭha; but Vasiṣhṭha baffled them all by raising a staff, imbued with his Brâhmaṇa energy, and all the Kshattriya might was humbled, and Vishvâmitra went away depressed and grieved. [§§. li-lvi.]

We may pause a moment on this production of material objects by the power of the will directed by the mind. The will, directed by the intelligence, has creative energy; even in common things thinking precedes formation; a man has an idea of an object before he makes it, a carpenter has an idea of a table before he shapes it. There seems to be a great difference between the carpenter who makes a table out of wood, and one who apparently makes it out of "nothing." But the latter does not make it out of nothing; he only does quickly what nature does slowly. The leaves of a tree draw gas out of the air, keep the solid part, rejecting the remainder, and build wood. The man who by the power of the will can manipulate the forces of nature gets out of the air the materials he needs, and builds them into the etheric shape produced by his thought. These things are possible now as of old, as I myself know, and when people laugh at the relation of them in old books, they only show ignorance. You must not be afraid of being laughed at: grow strong enough to disregard the laughter of the ignorant.

Vishvâmitra, humbled by a Brâhmaṇa, resolved that he would win the Brâhmaṇa power, would himself become a Brâhmaṇa, and he began to subdue his senses and practise austerities. At last Brahmâ, approving his efforts, hailed him as a royal Ṛishi, a Râjarshi, but Vishvâmitra was not content, and continued his efforts. [§. lvii.] After many toils, he gained another step, and was greeted by the Gods as Ṛiṣhi, but still continued his austerities, content with nothing short of becoming a Brâhmaṇa. But alas! he fell, for meeting an Apsarâ, Menakâ, he became a prey to passion, and recommenced his struggle, and was, after many years, saluted as Maharṣhi by Brahmâ, and bidden to strive to subdue his senses completely. On the next occassion of temptation. Vishvâmiṭra resisted an Apsarâ who tried to allure him, but he gave way to anger and uttered a curse against his tempter, and thus again failed. Still resolute, he took a vow of silence, determined to vanquish passion, and although every effort was made to provoke him, "yet could not anger enter his heart." At last he conquered, and was hailed as Brahmarṣhi, thus changing his caste from that of the Kshattriya to that of the Brâhmaṇa, and remaining for all time as type of the valiant man who hastens his own evolution by strenuous and persistent effort. [§§. lxiii.-lxv.]

A man only really belongs to a caste when the qualities of the caste are shewn in his character. A man of unchained passion, a man of angry speech, of impure life, of undeveloped intelligence, is not a Brâhmaṇa, though he be born in a Brâhmaṇa family a hundred times; a man who shews

Brâhmaṇa qualities becomes a Brâhmaṇa though he be not one by birth. The caste is not recognised by the Great Ones till the qualities of the caste are evolved, for true caste is in the inner man, not in the outer form. Where the two are found together, blessed is the man, happy is his karma; but when they are disjoined, better to have the lower form and the higher quality than the higher form and the lower nature.

Now was Râmachandra on the threshold of the great joy of His life. His studentship was over; by His conquest of the Râkshasas He had proved His manhood. Now He was to take up manhood's duties, to become a husband, a house-holder. This was the old order. No student was allowed to marry, but was under the vow of Brahmacharya. Till study was over, celibacy was imposed. And this for the soundest scientific reasons. The immature body cannot bear the double strain of hard study and of married life, and the result of placing this heavy burden on the shoulders of the student —according to modern custom—is weakened manhood and premature old age. Nature's laws—which are God's laws—cannot be disregarded with impunity, and modern India, in her enervated manhood, bears sadly eloquent witness to the karma entailed by the disuse of the ancient and wise law of Brahmacharya during the time of pupilage.

On the day following the telling of the story of Vishvâmitra, when king Janaka came to visit his guests, the sage asked him as to the wonderful bow of which they had heard, and begged him to show it to Râma. The king, in reply, told them that the bow had belonged to Shiva, and had been given by Him to the Gods at Daksha's sacrifice, and by the Gods to his own ancestor Devarâta. One day when he was ploughing a field, preparing it for sacrifice, a fair damsel sprang from the furrow, and that was Sîtâ, brought up as his daughter. He had promised her hand to any suitor who could bend the bow, and many kings and princes had striven to do so, but all had failed. [§ lxvi.] Then said Vishvâmitra; "Do thou show the bow unto Râma," and the bow was brought, borne on a great car, in a case garlanded with flowers. The sage bade Râma look at it, and He opened the case, and looking up with bright clear eyes, "Shall I lift the bow?" asked He. As both king and sage assented, Râmachandra took the bow from the case, and grasping it midway strung it, and then, as he drew the string, the bow snapped in twain, with a sound as of a thunder-clap. Thereon the king—when all had recovered from the astonishment caused by the strength of the youth who had so easily broken the bow no man could even lift—said to Vishvâmitra that Sîtâ, his fair daughter, was the prize of him that could bend the how, and now let king Dasharatha be sent for to bless the marriage of his son. [§ lxvii.]

Joyously king Dasharatha received the message of king Janaka, proposing the marrying of his two sons to the two princesses of Mithilâ, and after taking counsel with his ministers, he set out for Videha. Warm was the welcome he received, and preparations were made for the wedding of Râma to Sîtâ and of Lakshmaṇa to Urmilâ, the second daughter of the king. The daughters of king Janaka's younger brother, Kushadhvaja, were asked for as brides for Bharata and Shatrughna by Vishvâmitra and Vasiṣhṭha, so that the four brothers were wedded on one day. [§§ lxviii—lxxii.]

Then were spoken the famous words to be afterwards so nobly redeemed, as king Janaka placed in Râma's hand the hand of his daughter Sîtâ: "This Sîtâ, my daughter, do thou accept as thy partner in the performance of every duty; do thou take her hand in thine. May she be of loftiest piety, devoted to her husband, ever following thee like thy shadow." And as the four stately brothers with their gracious brides paced round the sacrificial fire, flowers fell from the sky and celestial music sounded, for

Lakshmî, in guise of earth's fairest maiden, had been joined on earth to Vishṇu.

On the following day, the marriage procession left Mithilâ for Ayodhya. To the surprise of all, as it went on its way, signs of disturbance arose on every side—the wind blew stormily, the earth shook, the sun was veiled in darkness, the air became thick with ashes. Then appeared through the gloom the terrible figure of Parashurâma, Râma of the axe, carrying a huge bow, and with his axe on his shoulder. Angry he seemed to be, and having been greeted by the saints leading the procession, he addressed Râma by name; saying that he had heard of the breaking of the bow, he bade Him string its fellow, the second bow made by Vishvakarman, the celestial architect, and given to Viṣhṇu, then by Viṣhṇu to Bhrigu's son, from whom it had descended to himself. Could Râma bend the bow of Viṣhṇu, as He had broken that of Shiva? If so, he would fight with Him. Then Shrî Râma lifted the great bow, strung it, and fixed an arrow to the string; but He paused ere loosing it, bethinking Himself that Parashurâma was a Brâhmaṇa, and that He might not strike him, even though challenged to the combat. Steadily gazing at the great ascetic, He asked him whether He should destroy his power of passing through the air, or the regions he had gained by his austerities. As the clear steady gaze of the younger Râma met his own, Parashurâma felt his own energy grow weak, for Vishṇu was drawing back to Himself the force He had embodied in the elder Avatâra, and he submissively bowed in worship before the slender youth, hailing Him as chief of the celestials, as Lord of the three worlds. His work was over. A greater than Râma of the axe was here. [§§ lxxiv—lxxvi.]

With his departure the sunshine returned, the procession was soon again on its way, and reached in due course the fair city of Ayodhya, gaily decked to welcome home the bridegrooms and the brides. Joyous was the greeting, loving the reception given by the happy mothers of the princes to their sons and their fair wives, and bliss reigned supreme in the palace of the king. Who then was happier than Râma with Sîtâ, passing peaceful days in duty and in love? Let the sun shine brightly on Them, for the clouds are not far off. [§ lxxvii.]

CHAPTER III.

Forest for Throne.

Bharata and Shatrughna now left Ayodhya to dwell with their uncle Ashvapati, leaving at home Shrî Râma and Lakshmaṇa—Râma who was now approaching the culminating point of His youthful glory. His character now shone out with extraordinary splendour, and was truly styled "incomparable on earth." Serene in soul and gentle in speech was He, never returning harsh answer to harsh word. One benefit called forth His gratitude, but a hundred injuries left no trace on His memory. He chose as associates the virtuous and the wise, and despite His strength and courage He was not proud. Truthful and learned, He showed deference to the aged, kindness to His father's subjects, pity to the miserable, sternness to the evil. He disliked improper talk, avoided all forbidden practices, and was pure in body as in mind. Discreet beyond His years and prudent, He was diligent, a judge of character, and sagacious in action. Versed in the Vedas, proficient in Saṁskrit and Prâkrit literature, Hė had mastered the learning of His time. Moreover He could ride and train horses and elephants, was a skilful archer, a brave warrior, and an able general. Such was the young prince who was the delight of king Dasharatha's heart, the pride of his subjects, the hope of the realm.

Little wonder that with such an heir, the king longed to see his peerless son definitely installed as successor ; so calling his nobles and princes round him he laid his wishes before them and took their counsel. (Ayodhyakâṇḍam, § i.) Aged was he and weary of the burden of sovereignty, and desirous to lay it down ; he wished for rest, installing Râma and yielding to Him the task of governing. Worthy was Râma to rule over the kingdom, worthy of loftiest trust. Let them speak their minds on the subject, and say whether they agreed or differed, for it might be that his wishes were ruling his judgment, and they might see some better way.

Very interesting is this glimpse of the olden times in the relations between monarch, princes and people. Having listened to the king, it is said, the Brâhmaṇas, the chiefs of the army and the citizens took counsel together, and, having come to a unanimous decision, they begged the king to instal Râma as heir-apparent. In answer to his doubt whether they so decided only to please him, they eloquently described the virtues of Râma, concluding by pressing him to "speedily instal thy son, endowed with noble qualities, resembling the God of Gods, ever intent upon the welfare of the whole State." [§. ii.]

Then the king gave orders that all should be prepared for the enthroning, and sounds of joyous preparation were soon heard on every side. In the midst of the glad turmoil, king Dasharatha sent for his son, who came, serene and stately, "with a countenance fair as the moon," through the shouting crowds, and, bowing low with folded hands, meekly embraced His father's feet. To Him the king announced the decision of himself and his counsellors, that He should be installed as heir and ruler, and wisely did the father advise his well-loved son: "Crowned with virtues as thou art by nature, yet, O my son, despite these virtues I will, for love's sake, advise thee for thy good. Practise increased humility and constantly control thy senses. Drive far away the ills that arise from passion and from lust. Replenish thy exchequer and thy arsenal; acquaint thyself fully, personally and through others, with the state of thy kingdom; administer justice, and thus win the love alike of nobles and of people; for the friends of him who rules the earth with satisfaction to his subjects, ever rejoice as do the Immortals when they drink the nectar. Therefore, O my son, disciplining thyself, do thou turn thy energies to thy task." No word of the glory and splendour of the kingly office, no encouragement to pride of pomp and power; humility, self-discipline, control of the senses, diligent discharge of duty—such were the virtues of kingship in ancient India. (§. iii.)

When all was ready, the king again sent for Shri Râma to tell Him that the morrow would witness His enthronement, and bade Him spend the intervening night in fast with Sitâ. So while all Ayodhya feasted and was glad, with "an uproar like the thunder of the rolling ocean when the moon is full," there was one house where only fast and prayer and silence prevailed—the house where prince and princess meekly prepared themselves to wear the heavy burden of a crown. (§§. iv.-vi.)

But there was another house in which a storm was gathering, a storm pregnant with disaster and ruin, and that house—strange to say—was the palace of the king. The citizens were decorating their homes and wreathing garlands along the streets; gay silks floated from door and window, till the city was glowing as a bed of gorgeous flowers; sandal-wood filled the air with fragrance, and music rang out merrily on every side; songs were heard resounding everywhere, and glad cries, "Râma is to be king! Râma is to be king!" How came it then that in the house of the monarch, to whom was due this joyous tumult, dark storm-cloud should gather, mutterings of grim disaster should be heard?

Seeing the preparations, a humpbacked woman of queen Kaikeyî's household, Mantharâ by name, asked the reason for them, and was told that Râma was to be enthroned as heir. Quickly she ran to her mistress, with whom she had grown up from childhood and whom she fondly loved, with a love too jealous to be wise, too partial to be just. To her she cried out angrily and loudly that Râma was to be installed in the kingdom, to her ruin and that of her son; whereupon Kaikeyî, overcome with joy at the news, gave her a splendid ornament as messenger of happy tidings, exclaiming: "Welcome is the news and dear to my heart. Difference feel I none between Râma and Bharata. Glad indeed am I that the king enthrones Râma in the kingdom." For dear was Shrî Râma to the hearts of His "three mothers," as He fondly called the three wives of His father, and to each He gave the love and reverence of a son.

But Mantharâ threw aside the golden ornament, and bitterly upbraided Kaikeyî with indifference to the welfare of her son. Bharata would be endangered by his brother's exaltation and she herself would become the slave of Kaushalyâ. But Kaikeyî, answering, praised Râma warmly, declaring that as eldest son the kingdom was His by right, and that He would guard His brothers as Himself. But Mantharâ, persisting, gradually worked subtly on Kaikeyî's mind by arguments, threats and persuasions, until at last she turned it wholly against the blameless Râma, and resolute to set Bharata in his brother's place. But how to work such a change? what method could effect such end?

Then Mantharâ reminded her that, long before, her husband having been sorely wounded, she had nursed him back to health, and he in gratitude, had granted her two boons. Those boons still remained unasked, and therein lay her power. Let her ask as one boon the installation of Bharata, as the other Râma's exile into the forest for fourteen years. Thus should Bharata have time to be firmly settled on the throne, and would keep it during his life. Let Kaikeyî go to the anger-room* and when the king sought her, let her be found weeping and sobbing; when the king was thoroughly worked up let her claim the boons, and then, after he had confirmed

* It is interesting to note that the modern word *boudoir*, a place in which to sulk, is the exact equivalent of this.

his promise, let her state the boons. Alas! Kaikeyî, torn with jealousy and suspicion, agreed to the plot, and began to act out the sorry drama. Going to the anger-room she flung herself on the ground, scattering round her the jewelled golden ornaments that decked her, and throwing away her costly royal robes; like a sorrowing beggar she lay prone on the hard bare earth, her beauty dimmed, awaiting the coming of the king. [§§ vii-ix.]

Meanwhile king Dasharatha, having completed his arrangements for the enthroning of Râma, bethought him that his best-loved queen, Kaikeyî, had not been told of the coming event, and he himself went to bear her the glad news. To his surprise, he learned from the sentinel that she had gone to the anger-room, and following her thither, he found her weeping on the ground. Stooping over her, he gently caressed her, and asked her grief, and with rising passion he poured out the wildest promises: who, though guiltless, should be put to death, or who, though guilty, should be spared? who, being poor, should be enriched, or who, being rich, should be made poor? King was he of earth's richest kingdoms, and all his wealth and power could grant was hers. Blinded by passion for this fairest and dearest of his wives, the king thus threw away all self-control, and wrought his own undoing. Then spoke Kaikeyî craftily, binding him fast: "I have a certain design which I long that you shall carry out. If you will do this, promise me, and then only will I reveal it." Taking her head on his lap, the king swore by Râma, dearest of all to him, that he would do her will, and thus in Râma's name doomed Râma to exile. Then Kaikeyî, calling the Gods to be witness to his oath, reminded the king of the two boons promised long before, and having bound him fast, "as a deer entering a noose," she uttered the fatal requests: Let Bharata be enthroned with the articles gathered for the enthronement of Râma, and let Râma, clad in deer-skin, go to the forest that very day, and there live as mendicant for fourteen years. The king had sworn. Let him perform his oath. (§§. x.-xi.)

Dismayed, overwhelmed, king Dasharatha sat, too late regretting his mad excitement, his easy fatal promise. Fainting he sank to the ground, swooning with grief and horror, and at last, overmastered by fierce anger, he broke out into wrathful upbraidings against Kaikeyî, and then grief-compelled fell into weak entreaties. The world might exist without the sun, but he could not live without Râma. Râma he could not renounce, all else might go. "I lay my head at thy feet. Be merciful to me," he wailed, in his desperate agony. "Have pity on me, aged and on the verge of death. O Kaikeyî, I fold my hands. I fall at thy feet. Be thou the protector of Râma, that I be not polluted by sin." Thus, careless of all dignity, all self-respect, the aged monarch wept at the feet of his wife. Obstinately Kaikeyî clung to his promise given, and would not yield, though again and again he implored her. How could he face Kaushalyâ, the ever tender and dutiful, whom he had neglected for the sake of Kaikeyî's beauty? How could Râma bear the forest life, quitting his happy home? What would befall the gentle Sîtâ, deprived of her husband's care? Râma would obey; he could not even hope that He would refuse to go, for He was ever dutiful. Kaikeyî was the destroyer of her race, the bringer of calamity, the causer of his infamy, who from weakness for his wife, would work the ruin of his blameless son. Thus in vain arguments, met ever by the obstinate answer, "Perform the promise given," the night wore away, and at the dawning a message came from Vasiṣhṭha, by Sumantra the charioteer, telling the king that all was ready, and praying him to summon Râma to the throne. The king remaining speechless, queen Kaikeyî bade Sumantra bring Râma thither, and as he hesitated, awaiting the permission of the king, Dasharatha said feebly: "Bring the noble Râma hither; I wish to see Him." Gladly Sumantra went to call the well-loved prince, knowing naught of what was behind the summons. (§§. xii.-xiv.)

The charioteer found the palace of Râma in festival, preparing for the splendid procession accompanying His going forth, and entering, saw Him seated with Sitâ standing beside Him, and delivered His father's message. At once Râma rose and set forth, Sitâ going with Him as far as the entrance, uttering fond wishes for His welfare, and He mounted the chariot awaiting Him, Lakshmaṇa following Him as he was wont. As He drove through the rejoicing crowds, glad welcome rang from every side, for was He not going to receive the empire, and all would be well when He was King. Arriving at the palace, He sought at once His father, and as He bowed in reverent salutation and saw His father sad, the one word "Râma!" coming from his lips like a groan, quick fear arose in the son's loving heart, and He asked Kaikeyî in hasty accents if in aught He had erred, had He through ignorance displeased him? Dryly the queen answered that he was not displeased, but he could not speak words that would pain his much loved son; it was for Râma to carry out what the king had promised and now shrank from performing; if Râma would perform what the king had promised, then she would reveal all, but the king would not speak. Sorely pained that it should be thought doubtful whether He would do His father's will, Râma answered quickly that He would spring into fire, drink poison, or plunge into water, if so ordered by His father and His king. "Speak, O honoured lady, the desire of the king, and I will carry it out. Râma does not go back from aught He speaks."

Then Kaikeyî bluntly told Him that when wounded in battle and tended by herself, the king had bestowed on her two boons. These boons she had now asked—the enthronement of Bharata, the exile of Râma for fourteen years. Bharata should then be installed with all the very articles brought for His own installation, while He should go to the forest, in bark, with matted hair, leaving Bharata, jewel-decked, to rule the earth. Let Râma redeem His father's word, and save the king from shame.

See! as the cruel sentence strikes Him, there is no change in the steadfast serenity on that peaceful face: "Be it as you say," He gently said; only He would fain know why His father was silent, he whose will was His law. Gladly would He yield Bharata the kingdom, or aught else; all was good that his father willed. "There is no virtue greater than service of the father, than carrying out his words." But Kaikeyî's own command would have sent Him to the forest, for she had full authority over Him. He would see His mother and comfort Sîtâ, and set forth that very day. So saying Shrî Râma saluted His father, and went on His way, and none saw change on His face as He passed homewards, though Lakshmaṇa followed with face black as thunder cloud. So well had Râmachandra learned the lessons of Vasiṣhṭha, so deeply had sunk into His heart the true Vairâgya, the sense of the utter worthlessness of all worldly things, that not even this shock of being flung from throne to forest, from sovereignty to beggary, from the height of worldly glory to the depth of worldly hardship, could move Him from His gentle serenity. But how would Sîtâ bear the news? What would His mother say? (§§ xv.—xix.)

Kaushalyâ was engaged in worship when Râma came to bring her the sad news, and grievous was her sorrow, bitter her lamentations. Unloved by her husband, she had been supported ever by hope in her son; if He were sent away, what remained? Maddened by Kaushalyâ's grief, by his brother's wrong, Lakshmaṇa broke in with angry burning words. Râma should not be exiled; his father was old and foolish, under the influence of his wife; let Râma seize the throne, and he would fight for Him, and would slay all who opposed. Kaushalyâ too forbade His going to the forest, for without Him she could not live. Between these two parents what should Râmachandra do? "There is no power in me," He said gently, "to transgress my father's order; low I bow my head to thee—I wish to go to the forest." Calming Lakshmaṇa's anger, pleading gently for his mother's permission—"Allow me to go, O venerable one, I shall return again after redeeming my father's promise"—excusing Kaikeyî for her cruel action, Râmachandra sought to win their assent to His departure. Over and over again He urged them to let Him go: "I shall abide by my father's orders;" and when Kaushalyâ declared, "Like unto a cow following its young one, shall I follow thee, O my darling, wherever thou shalt go," Râma tenderly reminded her of her duty to her husband, that she must not forsake him who was already deprived of his eldest son, and whose home was laid desolate. At last the sense of duty re-awakened in her heart, and Kaushalyâ yielded and bade Him go, redeeming His father's promise, coming back to her when the time of exile had expired. (§§. xx,—xxv.)

Yet one task remained; the strong gallant

heart had remained unshaken, though sorely pierced, while mother and brother had been racked with pain and anger ; now it most bear the heavier burden of the wife's anguish, for Sîtâ must be told of the exile of Her lord. Sîtâ was eagerly awaiting His return as the installed ruler of the kingdom, and when He entered, grave and silent, Her heart sank down with intuition of grief to come. Running to meet Him, She poured out eager questions: where was the royal umbrella that should shade Him, where the servants and the singers, the Brâhmaṇas and subjects, the chariot and the great elephant, the marks of royal pomp ? Gravely came the answer without preamble, confident in the strength of Sîtâ's heart: "O Sîtâ, born of a mighty race, versed in religion and wise, and devoted to pious rites, my father hath exiled me to the forest." Kaikeyî had claimed the promised boons, Bharata was to be king and He an exile. She must live peacefully at home, while He wandered afar, and serve His father and mother and His "other mothers" with respectful love ; She must seek to please Bharata, who was king both of the land and the family, and must obey his commands. "I am going to the forest, O my darling, and thou shalt live here." At this, Sîtâ broke in with loving laughter at the idea that Râma could be severed from her; the wife alone of all relatives shares the fate of her husband, and She was exiled with Him and would tread His path; She had done no wrong that She should deserve abandonment, and where Her husband was there only could She dwell. She had been taught to follow Her husband everywhere, and joyfully would She dwell beside Him in the forest, fearless of all danger, shielded by His strong arm. "Do thou accept my prayer, whose heart is wholly thine, knowing not another, ever clinging to thee, resolute to die if left by thee." So said She, smiling amid coming tears, incredulous of separation yet fearing it, wreathing soft arms round the neck of Her beloved, and pressing tender cheek on His. He, fearing the perils and hardships of the forest for His gentle darling, on whom rough wind had never blown, told Her of the dangers and the privations of such a life, and prayed Her to remain behind in the safe warm seclusion of Her home. But every peril painted to dissuade Her only made Her more resolutely bent to go, for should Râma face these dangers without Her, and she dwell in luxury while He lay cold and hungry? At last she burst into bitter weeping, crying that the thorns would be as soft as linen, dust as sandal, grass as blanket, roots and leaves as sweet as nectar, if only He were there.

"O Râma thy company is heaven and thy absence hell. Let me die at once if thou forsakest me. I cannot bear this grief for one brief moment; how then shall I live without thee for fourteen years?"

Then Râma caught Her closely to His breast, whispering that if She were thus resolved He could not say Her nay, and, His heart relieved of its worst strain, He bade Her distribute all Her possessions and prepare to follow Him. Then all the smiles came back, and gracious girlish laughter, as Sitâ despoiled Herself of all Her wealth to go as exile to the woods. (§§. xxvi—xxx.)

Then Lakshmaṇa, unable longer to restrain himself, caught his brother's feet and said that he too must go, meeting all Râmachandra's dissuasions with unshaken resolution. His it was to guard his elder brother and His wife, to search for Their food, to serve Them night and day. At length Shrî Râma again gave way, and sent Lakshmaṇa to fetch His arms of celestial workmanship, and when the brothers had distributed all their wealth and established their servants in security for the time of their absence, they set out to bid farewell to Dasharatha ere starting on their way. No longer through shouting joyous crowds, but through a lane of weeping woe-begone faces, the Three passed to the palace of the king, their faces the only serene ones in that vast concourse, their eyes the only ones not wet with tears. (§§. xxxi.-xxxiii.)

Arrived at the palace, they sought the king, who was sitting grief-stricken, and Shrî Râma prayed his permission to depart with Sitâ and Lakshmaṇa, begging him to instal Bharata, and to be content that his eldest son should redeem his pledged word. Happy and content would He be in the forest, serving His father there as before He had served him in Ayodhya. Let not His father sorrow; there was no cause for grief. Then Dasharatha bade the army be gathered, and all articles of luxury to go with Râma to the forest; but, true to the spirit of the promise, the hero would allow naught to be taken from His brother's kingdom, but would have only a vesture of bark in exchange for royal robes. Straight and tall and handsome stood the two splendid youths, clad in the ascetic garb so unfitted for their stalwart manhood, while Kaikeyî triumphed at the sight and the king gazed heart-broken. But when Sitâ's lovely form was shrouded in the ascetic dress, he could bear it no longer, and insisted that She at least should wear Her silken robes and royal ornaments, and so it was done, and again She shone forth in regal splendour.

Then Râmachandra prayed His father to treat tenderly His mother, who was "aged and famous and of a lofty spirit," now heart-broken at the loss of her son, and went forth after loving farewells, mounting with Sîtâ and Lakshmaṇa the chariot that was to carry Him away into exile. But outside were weeping crowds, and cries and lamentations rent the air, and the king and the queens rushed forth, following the car on foot. And the king and the people cried to the charioteer to drive slowly, while Shrî Râma urged him on to end the piteous scene, and as the horses sprang forward darkness fell, as though with the going of Râmachandra night had come. (§§. xxxiv.—xli.)

When the dust raised by the wheels of the chariot had disappeared, the king sank to the ground, but, raised by the faithful Kaushalyâ and supported by her, he tottered feebly towards his desolate home. Rejecting all aid from Kaikeyî, he bade them lead him to the room of Râma's mother, where alone his broken heart could rest, and there he lay stricken, with Kaushalyâ weeping at his side. (§§. xlii.—xliv.)

CHAPTER IV.

Brotherly Love.

The loving contest between father and son, the father trying to delay the son, the son striving to hasten away, was over. Râma was speeding forwards to the forest, but was still followed by crowds of the citizens of Ayodhya, unwilling to let Him go, even at the command of their king Touched by their affection, and seeing many aged Brâhmaṇas crying to Him to stop, He descended from His chariot, and walked beside them on foot, till darkness fell. Then, having arrived at the river Tamasâ, Râmachandra resolved to pass the night there, and while He slept peacefully beside Sîtâ, Lakhsmaṇa watched over His slumbers, talking of Him to Sumantra the Charioteer until the rising of the sun.

When Râma awaked, the citizens, worn out with fatigue and grief were still asleep, and he quickly bade Sumantra prepare His chariot, and forded the stream unperceived. Then He sent the chariot along a road leading in the direction He did not intend to pursue, and bidding Sumantra turn in his tracks carefully so as to veil them, and thus rejoin Him, they all set forth again towards the forest.

When the citizens awoke, lo! their loved Prince had disappeared, and seeking eagerly for Him, they found the track of the chariot wheels, but it led them only to an abrupt ending. Despairing of finding Him, no other trace being visible, they turned sadly homewards to that which was no longer home to them, now its sun had fled. And when they reached the fair city, it also was plunged in grief. The women were wailing as though their first-born sons were dead; the sound of music was hushed, the noise of trading had ceased, song and dance were nowhere found, the streets were dark and empty. So gloomy to His lovers does the world become when the light of Râmachandra is withdrawn. [§§ xlv.—xlviii.]

Where He was, however, all was well. Sîtâ was glad, at Her husband's side; Lakshmaṇa was content, guarding his much loved brother; Râma Himself was at peace, doing His father's will. And they fared onwards through the long day and the cool dusk night southwards, and left at sunrising the kingdom of Koshala, no longer His. When many hours had passed they reached the bank of Gangâ near Sringaverapura, and there, on the banks of the river, they decided to rest for the coming night. Then Guha, the king of the Nishâdhas, hearing of their coming, brought rich food and laid it at Râma's feet, but He gently answered, that the food given thus from love He accepted but might not enjoy, since He was bound by an ascetic vow, and could use naught save food for the horses. On the following morning He bade farewell to the faithful Sumantra, sending him home with many a loving message to those who wept His exile, and then, on a boat provided by Guha, He crossed the river with His wife and brother, placing the broad swift stream between Himself and His home. On the further side they spent their first night in loneliness, far from the haunts of men. [§§ xlix—liii.]

On the morrow, they set forth on foot towards Prayâga (Allahabâd), towards the spot where Gangâ and Yamunâ (Jumna) flow together, and there they found the hermitage of the famous Bharadvâja, and were welcomed gladly by the great ascetic. With him they spent the peaceful night, and then went on again, directed by him, to Chitrakûta, where Vâlmiki was dwelling; and there Lakshmaṇa built a wooden cottage and thatched it with leaves, and, having offered sacrifice and worshipped the Gods, Râma, His wife and brother entered with contented hearts their forest home. [§§ liv—lvi.]

Meanwhile Sumantra, with a heavy heart, had gone to Ayodhya, and there had sought the presence of the king. At first, the king was too overcome to speak, but recovering presently, he asked fondly after the welfare of his sons and of Sîtâ. Then the charioteer gave his son's loving messages, and related how Sitâ was happy, playing like a girl amid the trees and flowers, and fearless even of wild beasts, safe in the strong protection of Her husband; how his sons were contented in the forest life, and how Râma prayed His father not to think of them as unhappy, but to instal Bharata as ruler and to live in joy. But Kaushalyâ's heart could not bear to hear of her son in his exile, and, weeping, she bitterly reproached Dasharatha, forgetful of her duty to him and of his own grief. Then the king gently and sorrowfully, clasping his hands humbly, prayed her forgiveness, and she, ashamed, caught his hands and put them on her bowed head, begging him rather to forgive her own cruel words; and thus husband and wife were drawn nearer together by the gentle humility of the aged king.

For thus is the law, as to the overcoming of bitterness by sweet humility and patience. If in answer to Kaushalyâ's bitter words the king had answered bitterly, then would the quarrel have grown and grown, till a wide gulf had yawned between them. But he met her pride with humility, her reproach with meekness, her anger with tenderness, and thereby aroused in her also humility, meekness and tenderness, and peace came instead of strife. For the emotion felt by one person is aroused in another, and if the emotion be evil, the good man checks the answering evil in himself and awakens the opposite good emotion, and thus arouses in the first also the corresponding emotion of good. Let each try to do this himself, and quarrels will be checked and good will triumph.

On the following day the king related to his wife an early fault of his, caused by youthful vanity, the fruit of which he was now reaping in Râma's exile. He was a clever archer, and it was said of him that he could pierce his aim guided by sound alone. One day, hearing a sound which he mistook for the trumpeting of an elephant, he let fly an arrow, and pierced an ascetic who was filling his pitcher at a stream. Overcome with remorse on hearing his cry, he hastened to his side, but the ascetic was struck to death, and shortly after expired. Dasharatha went to the aged parents o carry the sad news of the slaying of their son, and led them to the corpse, and there the heart-broken father pronounced what is called a curse on the involuntary murderer of his son: "Thou shalt also find thy death from grief for thy son." Having said which he expired, together with his wife.

The pronouncing of a curse by an ascetic, or other pious man, is often referred to in the Scriptures, and it is well to understand the nature of such curses. Sometimes, indeed, they are uttered in anger, and then the utterer commits a fault, making bad karma for himself. But when they are uttered with deliberation and without anger, by one who knows the law and sees the future, they are simply the formal declaration of the result of the act then committed. If we inflict suffering on another, that suffering must inevitably return to us in the future. As an elastic spring may be stretched, but when loosed will spring back into its original form, so does every activity return to the actor. If we cause disturbance, it re-acts on us, the disturbers. As the ball thrown against a wall returns to the hand of the thrower, so does the act come back to the doer. The man who had broken a father's heart by the killing of his blameless son should himself suffer a broken heart by the loss of his own son, also blameless. But as the act was one of vanity and carelessness, not of malice, so should his own grief be a pure sorrow, unsoiled by sin. Nor did it long endure. For as the king finished his tale, and burst into lamentations for his son, his tired and broken heart ceased to beat, and he passed away from earth. [§§. lvii-lxiv.]

Through all these prolonged scenes of pain and sorrow there is one predominant fact that should be noted by every student. Blameless and stricken by what appeared to be an undeserved misfortune, Râmachandra was never for a moment deceived by this outward illusion of events and actors. He shows neither grief for Himself nor anger against others, but continually points out to those around Him that no one has done to them any wrong nor harm, but that all that comes comes by the Good Law. Suffering and happiness are severally the fruit of past demerits and merits, and no harm can be inflicted on any that is not the outcome of his own previous acts. Hence there is no reason for sorrow or for anger. None can injure another, save as the involuntary agent of the Law, which uses even men's passions as its servants, collecting its own debts by the hands that fancy they are grasping for themselves. This is one of the lessons that we should learn from the blessed life of Shri Râma, as true for us to-day as for the people of His own time. No debt can be exacted that we do not owe, and we should pay our debts like honest debtors. Why should we add to the original debt a new amount, made by our foolish resentment against the servants of the Law?

Great was the wailing that arose around the death-bed of the great monarch, and his counsellors gathered hastily and prayed Vasiṣhṭha to select from among the royal line the new king, for "as river without water, a wood without grass, a herd of kine without a keeper, is a kingdom without a king." Then Vasiṣhṭha reminded them that Dasharatha had conferred the kingdom on Bharata, who was living at his uncle's with his brother Shatrughna, and bade them send swift messengers to bring him home. But he counselled them simply to say that urgent business required his presence, and to speak no word of his father's death or of his brother's exile.

But Bharata had meanwhile received a hint that there was trouble in Ayodhya, for he had dreamed an evil dream, in which he had seen his father plunged into a dirty pool, and again in a car yoked with asses going to the south. From this he feared that his father, or one of his sons, was about to die. As he was telling his dream to his friends, the envoys came to call him home, and pressed him to start speedily. Rendered yet more anxious by this urgency, Bharata, taking leave of his relatives, set forth with his brother for the seven days' journey to Ayodhya, his heart heavy with fear; and his trouble became yet greater as he entered the city, and found silence and unswept streets and sad-eyed people, where before all had been busy and neat and joyous. Hurrying into the palace, Bharata entered his mother's rooms, and after saluting her he eagerly asked for his father, where was he, why was he not with her? Then Kaikeyî told him without preface that his father was dead, and despite all his forebodings, this confirmation of his fears struck Bharata to the ground, and he lay weeping, refusing to be comforted. Happy were Râma and those who had surrounded his father as he lay dying. But where was Râma, Râma who was now father, brother, friend, whose loving servant he was? To Râma he must go. But what were his father's last words? that he should first know. Then Kaikeyî told him that his dying father had spoken of the happiness of those who would see Râma return, with His wife and brother; and Bharata, puzzled, asked anxiously whither these had gone. And Kaikeyî answered smoothly that Râma had gone to the forest wearing bark, and Lakshmaṇa and Sitâ with Him. Then a fresh pang pierced Bharata's aching heart; his brother an ascetic, an exile, his sinless, peerless brother! could He, the sinless one, have sinned, that He should have been banished from the realm? But Kaikeyî quickly answered that Râma had done no wrong to any, but that she, his mother, had claimed the banishment of Râma and the kingdom for Bharata, in virtue of the hold she had upon the king. And she proudly bade him take the kingdom she had gained for him; let him perform his father's funeral rites and then assume the crown.

At this unexpected and most unwelcome news, Bharata sprang up like an angry lion, and poured forth a torrent of reproaches; she had exiled his brother, slain his father, and brought foul shame on him, making him usurp the place of his elder brother. "O enemy of mine in the guise of mother!" he cried in passionate anger; "do thou enter fire, or dive into Daṇḍaka, or wind a cord round thy neck; other desirable way there is none for thee." Vehemently he protested to the counsellors that he had never desired the kingdom, nor spoken to his mother about it; far away was he when the great crime was wrought. At this juncture, Kaushalyâ set out to meet Bharata, and he and Shatrughna met her, they having also started off to find her.

Kaushalyâ ironically complimented him on his gaining of the kingdom, and asked to be sent to the forest where Râma was; but was soon convinced of his innocence of the evil plot, and strove to comfort his passionate grief. Then Vasiṣhṭha came, urging him to perform his father's funeral rites, and summoning his self-control, the bereaved prince raised his father's body from the oil in which it had been preserved, and it was borne to the funeral pyre, and the rites for the dead were fully performed. [§§ lxv—lxxviii.]

As Bharata and Shatrughna were sadly speaking of Râma, as ill fate would have it, Mantharâ came into the room, gorgeously attired, blazing with jewels, expecting to receive praise from Bharata, for whom she had gained a throne. At the sight of her insolent splendour, his wrath blazed up furiously, and seizing her he thrust her before Shatrughna as the wicked cause of all their woe; let him deal with her as he would. Then Shatrughna, forgetting her womanhood in her wickedness, struck her down, and seizing her and pushing her in front of Kaikeyî, he bitterly reproached Bharata's mother, till Bharata, reminding him that these were women, bade him remember Râma's displeasure should even Mantharâ be slain, and so drew him away from the frightened women.

Now round him came the counsellors, the great men of the kingdom, praying him to seat himself on the empty throne, but firmly and sternly he refused. "In our race it hath ever been for the first-born to rule, and you who are wise should not urge me to transgress the rule. Râma, our eldest brother, shall certainly be king, and I will remain in the forest for the fourteen years." And he bade them call out the army, and set men to smooth the forest ways, that Râma might come back to his kingdom with all the pomp of royalty.

In vain was regal state offered to him: "I am not the king," was his steadfast answer. In vain did Vasiṣhṭha himself bid him assume the kingdom conferred on him by his father. "How should I deprive Râma of his kingdom?" was his grave reply. "He deserves the kingdom, just as Dasharatha did. I bow down to Râma, gone to the forest wilds. I will follow Râma. That best of men is king." Unshaken by all temptation, steadfast in duty, Bharata stood unmoved, resolute to serve and not to reign.

Joyous indeed was the vast procession that set

forth to lead Râma home, to hail Him King. Thousands of citizens went with the army, all talking with delight of Râmachandra's return. And they went happily onwards, till the broad stream of Gangâ barred their way. There Guha, king of the Nishâdhas, had prepared an army to stop their passage, fearing harm to Râma, but himself went to meet Bharata in order to find out what might be his intentions. Offering him a gift of food, he invited him to pass the night where he was, and in answer to Bharata's question as to the whereabouts of Bharadvâja's hermitage, Guha said gently that he knew well the place; but what intention had he as to Râma, for his vast army seemed to presage danger. Then with calm unclouded face, void of all evil intent, Bharata answered with quiet patience: "May the time never come when I shall do wrong to Râma. Thou shouldest not fear me. Râghava is my elder brother, dear to me as was my father himself. I go to bring back Râma, dwelling in the woods. Other thought have I none, and I speak truth, O Guha!"

Then Guha, delighted, praised Bharata, who was taking so much pains to give up a kingdom which had come to him without his seeking and could have been held by him unchallenged; "truly thy eternal fame shall spread over all the earth." And

Guha related to Bharata, greedy for news of his brother, how the exiles had spent the night, and showed him the bed of grass on which Râma and Sîtâ had slept, while Lakshmaṇa watched by them, bow in hand. You should read the pathetic account of Bharata's tender interest in all the details of his brother's hardships, hardships taken so lightly by the exiles themselves.

On the following day Bharata crossed Gangâ, and having encamped his army in the forest round Prayâga, Bharata himself went with Vasiṣhṭha, after putting off his armour and weapons, to visit Bharadvâja. Again, to Bharata's grief, he was accused of harbouring ill intentions to his brother, but, ever steadfast in patient meekness, he showed no resentment, but only repeated that he was going to bring his brother home. Then Bharadvâja blessed him, telling him that he knew his intention, and wished only to increase the firmness of his purpose, and bade him stay that night and rest with him. And then he desired him to bring his army, which, from respect, had been encamped at a distance, and he called on the heavenly architect, Vishvakarmâ, to come and build him lodgings for Bharata and his followers, and to various Deities to aid him in showing due hospitality. And from all sides they came, and made a splendid reception ground and rich repasts of every kind, and heavenly choristers and Apsarâs danced and sang, and charmed all hearts. So richly can a man give to others who asks nothing for himself.

On the morrow, directed by Bharadvâja, Bharata set forth again towards Chitrakûta, and arriving there his men began to search the wood, and presently caught sight of a column of smoke, shewing the presence of men. Hearing of this, Bharata stopped the search, and set forth himself with but two companions to seek his much-loved brother. [§§. lxxix-xciv.]

Meanwhile Râmachandra was living happily in the forest with His wife, His younger brother serving Them with faithful devotion. And one day as They sat taking food, a rush of frightened animals was heard, and Râma sent His brother to climb a tree and find the cause of the disturbance. And Lakshmaṇa cried loudly to his brother to arm Himself and place Sîtâ in safety in the cave, for behold Bharata was coming with an army to slay Them; angrily he shouted that he would now slay Bharata, for whose sake They were suffering exile. Gently Râma answered, soothing the anger born of love, that He wished for no kingdom stained by a brother's blood, for He would have no happiness that was not also that of His three brothers. Surely Bharata was coming out of love to seek Them, for never had he wronged his brothers, even in thought. Or if Lakshmaṇa himself wished to be king, Bharata, asked by Him, would place the kingdom in his hands. With quick repentance Lakshmaṇa cast aside his anger, and coming down from the tree, he entered the cottage with Râmchandra and Sitâ to await events.

Now Bharata with Shatrughna, and followed by Sumantra, was searching the wood, and presently came to the leaf-thatched cottage, and caught sight of Râma seated within upon the ground, with His wife and brother, His hair matted and clad in bark and deerskin. With a cry he rushed forward and flung himself at Râma's feet: "O noble one! O noble one!" he sobbed, choked by overmastering grief—Râma, worthy of earth's noblest kingdom, clad thus as poor ascetic, His royal locks matted, with deerskin for regal seat.

Then Râma clasped Bharata fondly in His arms, and lovingly asked him what had brought him to the forest, and where was their father; was he living or had he gone to the other world; surely the kingdom had not been wrested from Bharata, he being still young? Question after question, as to the welfare of the kingdom and as to Bharata's own diligence in ruling, poured from Râma's lips, overjoyed to see one coming from the land He loved so well. But why had Bharata come there, he who was a king, in deerskin and with matted locks like an ascetic—for Bharata had clad himself in ascetic wise and matted his hair, in token of his resolve not to wear the crown.

Briefly answered Bharata that their father, heart-broken, had gone to heaven, and that he himself had come to fetch home his brother, who must at once take His father's seat. Then Râma replied gently, but firmly, that his father had sent Him to dwell for fourteen years in the forest, while he had assigned the kingdom to Bharata : each must do his own work, obeying their father's will. For the moment Bharata evaded the issue, praying his brother to offer water and pinda to their father, and the four brothers with Sîtâ, going to the river-side, tenderly prayed for their beloved dead, and then, returning to the cottage, sat together, bewailing their loss.

Thither came Vasiṣhṭha, and the queens of Dasharatha, and re-united in the forest, mothers and sons again met, and passed the sad night together, one in grief as they had ever been one in joy. On the morrow, Bharata addressed his elder brother, bidding Him take the kingdom, which needed His strong protection. Râma, in answer, seeing his brother to be overcome with grief, spoke wisely on death, on its inevitableness, on its daily approach, and bade Bharata, while still life was his, so to act as to ensure his own happiness in the next world. But Bharata, praising Râma's calmness, made that very superiority new ground for His return as ruler ; only by becoming king could He free His father from sin, undo the evil wrought by Kaikeyî, release himself from the crime of ousting his elder brother. Warmly and vehemently he pleaded, but Râma remained unshaken, firm, unmoved. To Bharata's words were added others, and Vasishṭha himself, with all the authority of his sacred office, commanded Râma to assume the crown, declaring that, as his Guru, he assured Him that in so doing He would act rightly. But even by this highest authority Râma, firm in duty, could not be swayed. "What my father hath commanded must not be made untrue." Then Bharata declared that he would stay in the forest also, but Râma bade him return to his proper work, as neither of them must disobey their father. At length Bharata, falling at his brother's feet, prayed Him at least to appoint whom He would as regent of His realm, and Rama, praising him for his submission, bade His brother rule the land ; and on

Bharata's prayer, He gave him His gold-adorned sandals, sign and emblem of His royalty delegated for a while into His brother's hands. And Bharata swore that for the fourteen years of Rama's exile he would wear the cloth and hair of the ascetic, and live on fruits and roots outside the royal city, making the sandals the sign of the absent monarch, that the people might ever remember that Râma was their king. And thus in truth he did. For, returning to Ayodhya, he led the queens to the palace, and then himself departed to Nandigrama, where he proclaimed that he held the kingdom but in trust, and that the sandals representing the absent Râma, must alone be sheltered by the royal umbrella : when Râma returned he would himself replace them on Râma's feet and yield to Him His kingdom. Thus Bharata the dutiful ruled the land as Râma's regent, living as ascetic until Râma should return.

Bharata having gone, the forest life really began, for now everything was over and all possibility of the shortening of the exile was past. Râma, saddened by his brother's grief, was disinclined to stay longer in the place of such piteous memories, and travelled on further, visiting the famous ascetic Atri on His way. To the hermitage of Atri came also his wife Anasuyâ, herself a famous Yoginî, "worthy," said her husband, "of being bowed down to by all creatures." The aged woman and the fair and youthful Sîtâ held converse together, the great saint being highly pleased with the sweet gentleness and wisdom of the lovely girl, and, blessed by both husband and wife, Râma and Sîtâ went on Their way, accompanied by the ever faithful Lakshmaṇa. [§§ xcv.—cxix.]

They now entered the great forest of Daṇḍaka, the resort of many ascetics, but also much infested by Râkshasas. Going through the forest Lakshmaṇa went in front and Râmachandra behind, Sîtâ walking between them, but notwithstanding this, as they were thus walking, a fierce and mighty Râkshasa, Virâdha by name, suddenly rushing on them, seized Vaidehî and carried her off to a short distance, defying Her guardians to recover Her. In vain did Râma and Lakshmaṇa pierce him with arrows : they fell off from him as hailstones from a rock. At last letting go Sîtâ, he seized the brothers in his strong arms, throwing them over his shoulders, but soon found that he was only carrying his death. For, wrestling, they broke his arms and he fell to the ground, and they pounded him heavily till life was nearly fled. And then they dug a pit and cast him into it, while he, recognising Râmachandra, rejoiced that he was set free by Him from the curse of the Râkshasa form, into which he had entered to expiate a fault, and from which he joyously escaped as a prisoner from his cell.

The Râkshasa, ere dying, had advised Shrî Râma to visit the ascetic Sharabhanga, and to his hermitage the reunited three now turned their steps. As they approached his hut, they saw before it Indra, the King of the Gods, with many celestials round him, and Râma went forward alone, leaving Vaidehî with Lakshmaṇa. But Indra saw Him coming, and swiftly bade farewell to Sharabhanga—doing him homage, as the Gods ever do to great ascetics—saying that Râma was not yet ready to see him, and drove rapidly away through the air to Svarga. Then they approached the sage, and Râma asked his gnidance as to whither He should bend His steps, and Sharabhanga bade Him seek another ascetic, Sutikshna, and follow his advice. "Do thou now, my child," he concluded, "for a space look at me, while I leave off my limbs, even as a serpent slips out of his slough."

Then Sharabhanga built a fire and, after offering oblations with mantras, he entered the fire, which consumed his aged body, while he rose from it in a radiant form, youthful and splendid, and passed onwards into the heavenly worlds.

Now such a death as this sometimes raises

many doubts in the minds of people who do not understand the relations of what are called life and death. Rightly is suicide condemned, and when people read or hear of such a death as this, they ask : "How is it that a Sage commits suicide?"

For all ordinary people—men, women and boys—who are going along the road of evolution, suicide is to be regarded as a serious fault. A man finds himself in great trouble, perhaps he has committed some crime and fears detection ; he kills his body, to escape the result of his wrong-doing. Or a bitter disappointment befalls a man, and in grief he destroys his body. Or a boy, failing in an examination, throws off his body in a wild surge of pain and shame. In all these cases cowardice is at the root of the act, the desire to escape from blame or criticism, to avoid unpleasantness. He forgets the duties which surround him, and thinks only of his own escape. But so long as we have duties, duties to father, mother, wife, child, friends, our life is not our own and we may not do with it as we will. It is a part of the Great Life, with certain functions to perform. We may not, without failure in duty, cast it aside at our own pleasure. Nor as a matter of fact, can any one thus escape the results of his own actions. By killing the body, he only increases his sufferings, and finds himself in worse case than before.

But a time comes when evolution is finished, when a man's work is done, when all duties are discharged and karma is exhausted, when nothing else remains for him to do, and when his illuminated Spirit sees that the use of the body is over, and that no more service can be done therein. Under such circumstances a man who lives only as an instrument of the Great Life may rightly drop the body which is of no further service. But you would make a mistake if you regarded such a case as a justification for ordinary suicide, or if you suppose that any one can escape from reaping what he has sown by slaying his body.

As Râmachandra went on His way, Sîtâ, troubled in mind, gently questioned the wisdom of His carrying arms, He being there as an ascetic. To bear arms, she argued, causes men to think of fighting, and thoughts of fighting lead to the fighting itself. Indra, wishing to draw away an ascetic from the ascetic life, placed a sword in his charge, and as he carried it about, lest he should lose it, fierce sentiments invaded his mind and he left the path he was following. The virtues of the Kshatriya and that of the ascetic were different, and He was now living the ascetic life. On returning to Ayodhyâ, He would again practise the virtue of the Kshattriya. "I do not teach thee," said Sitâ sweetly; "I merely remind thee of this matter. Who can speak of righteousness to thee? Having thought, act as thou wilt." Wise and clever was her speech, in truth, and Râma praised her words; but Râmachandra had a deeper wisdom, and knew how to balance His duties. Not for Himself was He bearing arms, but for the defence of the ascetics who lived in peril of life, owing to the Râkshasas who ranged the forest. These ascetics prayed His protection, and He had promised it and could not break His word. "I had rather renounce my life, or thee, O Sîtâ, along with Lakshmaṇa, than my pledged word."

For ten years they lived in the forest of Daṇḍaka, wandering from place to place, seeing many a great Sage, and blessed and loved by all. There also He one day met a huge vulture, Jatâya, a friend of His father's, who promised protection to Sîtâ, while Râma went with Lakshmaṇa to seek a suitable dwelling-place. Having found it, Lakshmaṇa, building a spacious hut near the Godâverî, brought his brother and Sîtâ thither, and they dwelt happily for a while in this new home.

But the storm-clouds are again gathering on the horizon, and the great struggle of Râmachandra's life will soon be upon Him. [Áranyakâṇḍam, §§ i—xv.]

CHAPTER V.

THE CARRYING OFF OF SÎTÂ.

The winter had come, and the two brothers with Sîtâ were full of contentment in their forest home, Râma ever loving the winter season, and the others loving what he loved. Much of the past and of the future spoke the brothers, and one day Lakshmaṇa, referring to the past, wondered that such a woman as Kaikeyî should have been wife of Dasharatha and mother of Bharata. But Râmachandra checked him gently. "Do not, my brother, blame our second mother. Talk rather of Bharata." This is ever Shrî Râma's way. If any thing unkind is said He ever checks it, and speaks of good instead.

While they were seated in the cottage one morning, after bathing in the Godâveri and performing their morning worship, a Râkshasî, fearful to look upon and fierce, who was passing by, caught sight of Râma's splendid beauty and fell passionately in love with the princely youth. She spoke to him, enquiring why He was there, and He answered courteously, telling His name and lineage and the reason for His presence in the forest, and in turn enquiring who she was. She announced herself as Shurpaṇakhâ, a Râkshasî, sister of Râvaṇa, as well as of Kumbhakarṇa, Bibhîshaṇa, Khara and Dûshaṇa. Let Râma become her husband, casting off this ugly thin Sîtâ, and He should range the forest with her at His will.

Then Râma said, laughing, that He was married, but there was Lakshmaṇa available for her, why not take him? He was young and beautiful and worthy of such a bride. Shurpaṇakhâ was nothing loth, but Lakshmaṇa merrily declined the match, on the ground that he was dependent on his brother, and he assured her that his brother would certainly renounce the lean and ugly Sîtâ in favour of such a paragon of beauty as herself. The Râkshasî then, turning back to Râma, rushed upon Sîtâ to devour her, and Lakshmaṇa, quickly interposing, struck off her nose and ears, sparing her life, and Shurpaṇakhâ fled away shrieking, and came to her brother Khara, to whom she poured out her woefull tale. There were two brothers, intruders in the forest, and with them a woman, for whose sake they had injured her. Now she would have them slain and would drink their blood. Then Khara furiously called to fourteen of his followers, and bade them slay the human intruders, and they started with the speed of the wind, guided by Shurpaṇakhâ, but only to meet death at the hands ot Râma, after He had vainly remonstrated with them, urging them to desist. Shurpaṇakhâ again flies to Khara, who, yet more enraged, calls his brother Dûshaṇa with a huge army, and himself mounts his war-car to accompany them to the combat.

Meanwhile Râma had sent Sîtâ for safety to a neighbouring cave, under the protection of Lakshmaṇa, and stood alone, clad in shining armour and bow in hand. From every side the dark opposing hosts bore down upon Him, the solitary radiant warrior, and rolled back broken and shattered, as waves breaking against a rock. At last Dûshaṇa engages Râma in conflict and falls slain to earth, leaving but two chiefs, Trishira and Khara himself. Ere long, Trishira had fallen, and a duel between Râma and Khara ends in the slaying of the latter, leaving the solitary warrior master of the corpse-strewn field.

But now a mightier foe was to be stirred up, the brother of Dûshaṇa and Khara, the mighty lord of Lankâ, Râvaṇa, the Ten-Headed.

This was the foe to meet whom Vishṇu had become incarnate as Râma. Slowly the threads of

Râma's life had been drawn to bring about this meeting, and the hour was drawing near when their lives should cross.

Now Râvaṇa had behind him a strange story. Greatest of Râkshasas he now was, but of far other than Râkshasa does this story tell. For he had been a devotee, one of the greatest of devotees both to Mahâdeva and to Vishṇu, a Bhakta of the Bhaktas. Learned also was he, wise in the science of the Self, versed in the Vedas above all others, a store house of Vaidik knowledge. He had climbed up to Vishṇu's heaven, and there with a fellow-devotee, acted as gate-keeper, Jaya and Vijaya their names. As gate-keeper he refused admittance to heaven to one who had the right of entry, and as a punishment he was obliged to choose one of two alternatives; would he be born seven times on earth, leading ever a blameless life of pure devotion, or would he be born three times only, but as enemy of Vishṇu, gathering up under himself earth's evil in order that it might he destroyed. Seven births as Ṛishi, or three births as Râkshasa—which would he take? Then, because he loved his Lord, and because every year of exile from Him was the torture of hell, he chose the three births of enmity rather than the seven births of love, and he was here on earth for the second of these births as Râvaṇa, conqueror of Gods and men, ruler of the Râkshasas, terror of the saints.

As Vijaya had been associated with Jaya in the refusal to admit, so was he in the births of expiation, and they were born as brothers in each of these, and in each were destroyed by two divine manifestations. They were born first as Daityas—as Hiranyâksha, who carried the earth below the waters, and who was slain by the Avatâra Varâha, and Hiranykashipu, father of Prahlâda, slain by the Avatâra Narasimha. Then they came as Râkshasas—as Râvaṇa, slain by the Avatâra Râma, and Kumbhakarna, slain by His brother Lakshmaṇa. The final incarnation was of men—as Shishupâla, slain by the Avatâra Kṛishṇa, and Dantavaktra, slain by His brother Balarâma.

To this Râvaṇa, king in Lankâ, came hastily Akampana, a Râkshasa, who had been dwelling with Khara in Janasthâna, and told him all that had happened.

At once Râvaṇa exclaimed that he would himself go and slay Râma, but Akampana, dissuading him from combat, craftily suggested that he should rather bear away Sîtâ, the matchless wife of Râma, for Râma, whom none might slay in battle, would swiftly perish of grief were Sîtâ rapt away. This plan delighted Râvaṇa, who at once ordered out his car, and drawing swiftly through the air northwards, he stayed his chariot at the dwelling of Mârîcha, who, it will be remembered, had felt the might of Râma's boyish arm. Earnestly and gravely Mârîcha prayed Râvaṇa to abandon his mad project, and not seek his own destruction by touching the beloved of Râma's heart; and for the moment, persuaded by his friend, Râvaṇa desisted, and went back quietly to Lankâ. [§§ xvi—xxxi.]

But thither came Shurpaṇakhâ, demanding vengeance for her own mutilation and the slaying of her brothers and their hosts, and she bitterly reproached Râvaṇa for his supine inaction while Râma was driving out his subjects and harassing his fastness Janasthâna. "Who is Râma?" cried Râvaṇa furiously, and Shurpaṇakhâ described the gallant youth and Lakshmaṇa His brother, and then craftily went on to praise the beauty of Sîtâ, in terms calculated to awaken Râvaṇa's passion; surpassingly lovely was She, Her skin like burnished gold, Her form graceful, Her beauty unparalleled on earth. Fit wife was She for Lankâ's lord; let Râvaṇa go forth and carry Her away, thus avenging his brothers and their hosts. [§§xxxii-xxxiv.]

Fired with fierce desire to possess the peerless Sîtâ, Râvaṇa issued forth once more, and again sought Mârîcha, but this time with imperious all-compelling will. Briefly he narrated the slaughter of the Râkshasas, and declared his resolve to carry off Sîtâ. But he needed Mârîcha's help. He must become a golden deer and play about the cottage of Râma till Sîtâ prayed Her husband and brother to capture the lovely creature, and then he would himself swoop down on the helpless Sîtâ, and carry her away. Terrified, Mârîcha listened to the plot, and then once more strove to dissuade Râvaṇa from rushing into the open mouth of death. Sîtâ was dearer to Râma than His life, and He was of strength incomparable, and of noble character; none could face Him in wrath and live. Then he related how Râma had struck himself at the sacrifice of Vishvâmitra, but had spared his life, and how later again he had attacked Him in ignorance, and had escaped once more, and that since then Râma had become a terror to him, and he saw Him everywhere, on every side, waking and sleeping. Sternly Râvaṇa answered he had not asked for counsel but had commanded service as Mârîcha's king. Truly there was a risk to Mârîcha in the undertaking, but if he refused obedience he should forthwith be slain. Thus threatened, Mârîcha gave way, and mounting with Râvaṇa into the air-chariot, he soon arrived in the forest of Daṇḍaka.

There he quickly, by the Râkshasa power of illusion, took shape as a lovely deer, golden skinned and silver-dappled, with jewelled horns and sapphire belly, and tail flashing with rainbow hues. He played amid the trees and mixed with the forest deer, but see! the wise wild creatures sniff a foe, and fly in every direction as he comes. But Sîtâ is less wise, less wary, and is captivated by the beauty of the gleaming gems. "Come quickly, come quickly," She cried aloud to Her husband and His brother, and they came at Her call. But Lakshmaṇa, who was so true himself that he detected falsehood at a glance, said to Râmachandra: "This deer is the Râkshasa Mârîcha: there is no such deer on earth. Pure illusion is this, O Râghava." But Sitâ shortly contradicted him, and full of excitement, urgently begged Her husband to catch the deer, alive if possible, but to get it at all hazards—for She was under the influence of enchantment, and had lost Her self-control. Then Râmachandra, yielding to Her eagerness, bade Lakshmaṇa stay with Sîtâ and guard Her, while He, at Her bidding, went to chase the golden deer. And thus Râma and Sîtâ parted, not to meet again for many a weary day.

On went the jewelled deer, darting hither and

thither, now near at hand, now far away, ever beguiling Râmachandra further and further away from His forest home. At last, Râma's arrow pierced it, and Mârîcha, to win Lakshmaṇa away from guarding Sîtâ, cried aloud in dying, with Râma's very voice: "Ah Sîtâ! Ah Lakshmaṇa!" as though Râma cried aloud for help in agony.

That piteous cry reached Sîtâ's anxious ears, and passionately She implored Lakshmaṇa to hasten to his brother's aid. "Save thy brother, who is crying aloud in the forest." But Lakshmaṇa remembered his brother's order, and did not leave Her side. Maddened with fear, and losing all sense of justice in Her love, She turned on Her faithful guardian with bitterest reproach. He wished Râma's destruction, he was His enemy in garb of a brother, being moved by desire for His wife. Ever clear-sighted and loyal, Lakshmaṇa answered gently that none could defeat Râma; the cry was but an illusion of Mârîcha's. She was left in his charge by Râma, and he did not dare to leave Her. But she answered again, pressing Her cruel reproach, declaring that he was moved by lust, coveting his brother's wife, that he had been plotting to obtain Her, and therefore had followed Râma to the forest. Pierced to the heart that loved Râma better than its own life, and respecting his brother's

6½

wife even when She was thus glamoured by the power of the Râkshasas, Lakshmaṇa answered sadly: "Thou art a very Goddess unto me; I therefore dare not answer thee." But thus were women ever. "I shall go where Râma is; may the deities of the forest protect thee." Low he bowed before Her and turned away, yet as he went he glanced back again and again, to see if She would repent and call him back. But She stood silent, and, as Lakshmaṇa disappeared, Râvaṇa stood before Her. [§§xxxv—xlv.]

Clothed as an ascetic, with triple stick and water-vessel, the fell Râkshasa in winning guise approached and addressed her. Praises of her beauty, all unfit for ascetic lips, flowed freely from his flattering tongue, while Sîtâ brought water and food, silently signing him to partake, and glancing anxiously round for Râma and Lakshmaṇa. But only the spacious forest land stretched wide on every side: neither husband nor brother was in sight. At last, fearing to anger this apparently saintly guest by silence, Sîtâ spoke, telling Her name and the occasion of Her being in the forest, and praying the guest to rest a while, as Her husband would return in a moment.

Then Râvaṇa threw off his disguise, impatiently

worn, and declared his name and purpose, urging her to fly with him to Lankâ, where she should reign in luxury as queen. At this Sîtâ's high courage awoke, and She looked as an angry lioness, as She answered Her insulter. Râma's was She, and His alone. Would he draw a lion's teeth, or a serpent's fang, would he drink poison, or lick a razor with his tongue, would he bind a fire with a cloth, or tread on iron spikes? Safer were these, than to touch Râma's wife. But Râvaṇa, deeming that where flattery failed, terror might succeed, spoke sternly and meaningly: Râvaṇa was he, the Ten-headed, whom all the celestials feared. The wind dared not blow on him, the sun for him softened his fierce rays, rivers stopped their running, the forest leaves were paralysed and dared not move. Râma was but man, and he lord of the Râkhasas, reigning in unchallenged might. But though he might terrify earth and heaven, Râvaṇa could not terrify this frail woman, loyal to Her lord. "One might still breathe on earth after carrying away the wife of Indra, but none may hope to live in peace who steals away Râma's love." Then Râvaṇa, furious, assumed his own gigantic form of terror, and, seizing Sîtâ, he mounted with her into his air-chariot and fled swiftly southwards. In vain Sita's cries for help rang through the air. In vain She called on

Lakshmaṇa, so lately driven from her side. In vain She shrieked to Râma, sent after the golden deer. She cried to the river, to the trees, to the deer, to the birds and forest creatures, to tell Râma that Râvaṇa had stolen away Sîtâ and catching sight of Jaṭâyu, king of the vultures, She implored him to carry to Râma and to Lakshmaṇa the news of the dire fate that had befallen Her. [§§xlvi—xlix.]

Jaṭâyu suddenly roused from sleep, spoke softly and beseechingly to Râvaṇa, reminding him that Sîtâ was wedded wife, and that it was foul crime to steal away the wife of another. And as Râvaṇa showed no sign of yielding, but on the contrary rushed at him in attack, Jatâyu, old as he was, engaged in conflict, in the hope of delivering Sîtâ from his grasp. But vain were all his efforts and after a long and furious struggle, in which Râvaṇa's car was wrecked, he fell to the ground, his wings cut off bleeding and dying.

Again Râvaṇa rose in the air with his victim, and as he fled Her bangles fell to the ground and Her golden breast-chain; and a little further on She saw five monkeys, and threw down near them Her cloth of yellow silk and jewelled ornaments, hoping that they might take them to Râma, as tokens of the direction of Her flight. And, carrying "Sîtâ on his lap, representing his own death," Râvaṇa entered his own city of Lankâ and placed Sîtâ securely in his house. [§§. l.-liv.]

When he thought She had realised Her helplessness, separated from Her husband by a broad ocean and alone amid encircling foes, Râvaṇa sought the weeping Sîtâ and forced Her to go with him to see the treasures of his palace. He showed Her the golden and crystal pillars, the ivory and silver windows, the inlaid diamonds and countless gems. He led Her through lovely gardens, studded with tanks and musical with the song of birds. He offered Her servitors by thousands, superb ornaments, the enjoyment of rule over all. He placed on Her feet his proud head—"Ravana has never before bowed his head to any woman." Stubborn against all his pleadings, blind to his gifts, deaf to his flatteries, Sîtâ remained unmoved. Quietly She told Râvaṇa that he was bringing destruction on himself, his city and his hosts, and that he could not turn Her from Her faith. Enraged at Her resistance, Râvana told her furiously that if She did not yield to his will, he would have Her slain for his morning meal, and calling some Râkshasîs, he delivered Her into their hands, bidding them take Her to the Ashoka wood, and by terror, or by persuasion, win Her to his will. Then Brahmâ, moved by pity, sent Indra to console Her, and he gave Her celestial food, so that Her strength might not fail. And She took it, after offering it to Râma and Lakshmaṇa in Her heart, and soothed and comforted, rested in peace. [§§. lv. lvi.]

Now Râmachandra, having slain the golden deer, was hurrying homewards, ill at ease as to Sîtâ, fearing that she might have heard Mârîcha's dying cry. What was His distress when He met Lakshmaṇa, looking sad and troubled, and He gently blamed him for having left Sîtâ. But was Sîtâ living, or had he come, She being dead? Quickly hurrying onwards, they reached the hermitage, only to find it vacant, and as Râma still blamed His brother deserting his charge, Lakshmaṇa related what had happened, and how She had taunted him with base designs. Sadly Râma blamed him for being moved by the words of an angry woman, thus leaving Her unprotected. Rushing in every direction, He searched the neighbouring thickets, asked every tree in piteous accents for news of His beloved, and called on deer, elephant and tiger to tell Him if they had seen His heart's delight. "Sîtâ! Sîtâ!" He cried, "art thou hiding, art thou playing? Oh come, such sport is my death!" But only silence answered Him, and His heart told Him that Sîtâ was not there. To the river Godâveri they went, but the rippling stream gave them no message of Her fate. Back to the forest they ran, still searching, and meeting a herd of deer Râmachandra cried again to them, "Where is Sîtâ?" And they, who had seen her carried away by Râvaṇa, turned to the south, raising their heads towards the sky, and the brothers turned in that direction and presently found signs of a bloody conflict, the conflict between Jaṭâyu and Râvaṇa. And Râma, becoming distraught with grief at seeing amid the wreckage parts of Sîtâ's garlands and some broken ornaments, put to his bow-string some flaming arrows, threatening to destroy the world. But Lakshmaṇa spoke softly in gentle dissuasion: "Ere this thou hadst been gentle, self-controlled and engaged in the welfare of all beings. It doth not befit thee now to abandon thy nature, overcome by wrath. It beseems thee not to destroy the world for the fault of a single person." Gently, tenderly he pleaded, till Râma regained His calm, and began again His search.

Ere long the brothers came on Jaṭâyu, the heroic vulture, lying covered with blood, and for a moment Râmachandra suspected him of being concerned in Sîta's death. But Jaṭâyu quickly told him of his fight with Râvaṇa, and how the great Râkshasa, slaying him, had gone southwards with the wailing Sîtâ. And then the royal bird, his mission discharged, fell over, dead, and the brothers, after burning his body, went on once more with their sad search. [§§. lvii-lxviii.]

Meeting a monstrous Râkshasa and being assailed by him, the two young warriors cut off the arms that gripped them, thus unwittingly releasing him from a curse; at his prayer, they burned his Râkshasa body, and from the fire he arose in his own proper form, Kavandha, the beautiful son of Danu, and bade them seek Sugriva, a monkey chief, son of Sûrya, who had been driven away from home by his brother Vâli, the son of Indra; with this monkey should Râma make a vow of friendship, and he would send out monkeys to search everywhere for Sîtâ, and these would surely find her. He then described to Râmachandra the path He should take through the forest to find Sugriva, bidding Him visit on the way a pious female ascetic, Savarî by name, in order that she might gain liberation. And saying again, "Do thou make friends with Sugriva," Kavandha, shining with celestial beauty, vanished from sight.

Onwards went the brothers, according to his directions, finding Savarî, who had collected fruits for their refreshment, having been told of their coming by the ascetics whom she had served till they left their bodies. Then, with Râmachandra's permission, she entered the fire, and rising from it in a body of light she soared upwards, following her beloved teachers to the higher worlds. But the brothers, still bound to earth by duty, went on through the forest, and reached presently the fair lake of Pampa. [§§. lxix.-lxxv.]

CHAPTER VI.

SÎTÂ'S FAITH.

You will remember that when Vishṇu decided to come down on earth, in answer to the prayer of the Gods, many of the Gods were directed to produce beings who should take shape as monkeys and bears, to help Râmachandra in the hour of His distress. These beings were able to change their shapes at will, and were semi-divine creatures, not the ordinary animals going by these names, wielding in animal forms superphysical powers. It is a characteristic of the Hindu religion that no sharp line of demarcation exists between men and animals, and that the animal form is taken as readily as the human for the purposes of divine manifestation. For men, animals and plants are not really separated independent kingdoms, but are equally manifestations of one all-embracing Life. And it is well that we should realise that whether one form or another veil it, the life is still the one Life, the divine, and that we should therefore recognise and respect it in all forms, worshipping it everywhere, not holding ourselves apart as having a right to use without being used, but seeing our own lives as links in one chain of existence, supporting others and being supported by them. The result of this recognition should be kindness to all creatures, and if this virtue has much diminished in India, it is because the old ideals have lost much of their power, and men think that the human form makes its owner the irresponsible tyrant of the lower races, using power to oppress instead of to protect.

When the brothers reached the lake of Pampâ, the very beauty of the scene, the limpid water, cool breeze and fragrant blossoms, led to a fresh outburst of grief from Râma for the sweet companion of happier hours, hours when They sported in just such scenes, and found all beauty doubled when seen by both together. Then Lakshmaṇa gently recalled Him to patience and effort ; "Do not grieve thus, O best of men. Even sinless ones lose their senses when overcome with grief. Console thyself, and abandon this weakness of heart. Lacking sufficient efforts even strong men do not regain lost objects. Mighty is energy, and there is on earth no greater force than this. There is nothing unattainable to one who is gifted with energy." And Râma, encouraged by the calm steadfastness of His brother, shook off His grief and again turned His mind to duty.

Meanwhile the approach of the two stalwart youths in warrior-array was much troubling the minds of Sugriva and his friends, and Sugriva, fearing that they were sent by his brother Vâli, became greatly terrified. For Sugriva was not, on the whole, a very gallant monkey, and readily showed signs of terror when danger threatened. But Hanumân, son of the Wind-God, cleverest of counsellors, bravest of warriors, consoled his chief in wise words, and readily undertook to go to meet the young warriors, and enquire as to their intentions. Then he changed his form into that of an ascetic, and, approaching the brothers, he greeted them courteously, enquiring their names and purpose, and announcing himself as the counsellor of Sugriva, Hanumân, a monkey, coming to them on behalf of his chief. His sweet words much pleased Râmachandra, who bade Lakshmaṇa reply to him in fitting words, expressing his admiration of the skilful envoy and praising the good fortune of his master. Then Lakshmaṇa answered Hanuman, expressing their good will towards Sugriva, and presently explained to him all their purpose, and that they were seeking the aid of Sugriva in order to find the lost Sîtâ. Hanumân, hearing this, was much delighted, for he thought within himself that these gallant warriors might enable Sugriva to gain his brother's throne; and changing his form to that of a gigantic monkey, he raised Râmachandra and Lakshmaṇa on his back and swiftly bore them into the presence of Sugriva. To the monkey chief he briefly explained the situation, and then Râmachandra and Sugriva, both in need of the other's help, clasped hands and walked around the fire, thus vowing friendship to each other. Then, each delighted at his gain, they sat together and began to talk. [Kishkindhâkâṇḍam, §§ i.—v.]

Sugriva told Râmachandra that he had lately seen a lady borne away by Râvaṇa, crying on Râma and Lakshmaṇa, and that she had dropped her scarf and ornaments, which he had picked up and preserved. Bringing these from a cave, he held them out to Râma, who, recognising his wife's jewels, caught them to His bosom, weeping. "See, Lakshmaṇa," He cried, "see this scarf and these ornaments which Vaidehî has let fall!" Lakshmaṇa's answer is full of the tender reverence in which he had ever held his brother's wife. "I do not know Her bracelets; I do not know Her earrings. But I know full well Her bangles, from ever bowing down unto Her feet." Never had he raised his eyes to face or arms, but he knew the jewels that decked the slender ancles of the feet he had so oft saluted.

Then Sugriva promised that he would aid Shrî Râma in recovering his wife, and gently sought to console Him, and Râma, comforted, promised that He in turn would aid His new-found friend.

On the following day Sugriva related his story to the brothers, and told him how he had come to quarrel with his own brother. Vâli had been placed on the throne, as the eldest son, on their father's death, and a quarrel arising between an Asura named Mâyâvi and Vâli, Mâyâvi one night challenged Vâli to fight him. Vâli went out, followed by Sugriva, and the Asura fled, and after running for some distance entered a large cave. Vâli bade his brother remain at the mouth of the cave while he pursued the Asura, and Sugriva remained there on guard for a year. He then began to think that his brother must be dead, and, seeing some blood flowing out from the cave, he concluded that the Asura had slain him, and rolling a large stone to the mouth of the cave, he thus closed it and returned to Kishkindhâ. There the counsellors installed him as king in his brother's place. Meanwhile Vâli, instead of being killed, had killed the Asura, and was very angry to find his exit blocked when he returned to the mouth of the cave, and still more angry to find his brother in possession of his throne. Rejecting all Sugriva's excuses, he banished him from the kingdom and took possession of his wife, and Sugriva had since been wandering as a homeless fugitive. Now he hoped that by Râma's power he might overcome his brother and take his throne.

Encouraged by Râma, Sugriva challenged his brother, and a furious struggle took place between them in which Sugriva was worsted and fled. Râmachandra stood by, bow in hand, but took no part in the conflict, and, when reproached by Sugriva, answered that the brothers were so alike that He could not distinguish one from the other, and was afraid of wounding His friend. He bade him put on a garland and again challenge Vâli, and then would He shoot the latter. According Sugriva once more roared out his challenge, and Vâli, hearing the sound, sprang up to meet him. In vain did his wife, Târâ, seek to hold him back, telling him that Sugriva was not brave enough thus to challenge him unless backed by some powerful friend, and that she had heard from Aṇgada, her son, that the princes of Ayodhya, Râma and Lakshmaṇa, had come to the forest, and were probably helping Sugriva. Let Vâli make friends with his brother, calling him home and declaring him his successor on the throne. Thus wisely and tenderly pleaded Târâ, fearing for her husband's life.

But Vâli, answering lovingly, said he could not manfully refuse a challenge, but he would not fight with Râma, nor would he slay his brother. Issuing forth he rushed upon Sugriva, and the brothers again fought with each other. Once more Sugriva was worsted, but Râmachandra set an arrow to his bow, and striking Vâli full on the chest, felled him to the earth. As he lay there dying, and Râma came to his side, he spoke gently but boldly in calm reproach; Why had He mingled in a conflict that was not His, striking down a warrior battling with his foe? Was this a righteous act, worthy of a Kshattriya? He had done Râma no wrong, offered Him no insult. Why had He slain him, a monkey, engaged in battling with one of his own race? There was no need to be sorry for him, since all must die, but what could Râma answer, when questioned on his death? Râma answered gravely that that land belonged to His own royal line, and that by its rulers justice was administered to all who dwelt therein. He had taken his brother's wife, and for that base crime He, representing king Bharata, had punished him as a criminal, not fought with him as a warrior. Then Vâli, confessing his crime, accepted his death as fit punishment, and prayed Râma to guard his only son, Aṇgada; while Târâ, hearing of his fate, came hastily with Aṇgada and threw herself on her dying husband, bewailing him with tender and loving words. And the dying chief spoke lovingly to his brother, bidding him take the kingdom and guard, as his own, the young prince now left fatherless; then, with a few wise words of counsel to his son, he died. Sugrivâ, his object gained, was now overwhelmed with remorse for his brother's death, while Târâ prayed Râma to slay her also, that she might accompany her husband to the heavenly world. But Râmachandra consoled her gently, and bade them cease from the lamentation that did not tend to the welfare of the deceased: Vâli had passed on into a happy world, won by his own good deeds; let lamentations cease, and the funeral ceremonies be performed.

These having been carried out with pomp, Hanumân prayed Râmachandra to instal Sugriva as king, and Râma bade the counsellors instal him and recognise Aṇgada as heir. And this was duly done in the city of Kishkindhâ, which Râma refused to enter, bound by His vow, and He bade them dwell in peace there through the rainy season, while He abode in the forest with Lakshmaṇa, dwelling in a cave, until the rains had ceased and the search for Sîtâ could be again pursued. [§§vi—xxviii.]

The rainy season over, Hanumân urged on Sugriva his duty to Râma, which he was forgetting in his own enjoyments, and Sugriva thereupon issued orders to collect the monkey hosts, but himself made no exertion to begin the great undertaking of the recovery of Sîtâ. So Râmachandra, who said piteously that the four months of rain had seemed to Him like a hundred years, bade Lakshmaṇa go to Sugriva and recall him to his duty, but use soft words and not give way to anger—for Lakshmaṇa had hastily declared that he would slay Sugriva as a liar. So Lakshmaṇa went to Kishkindhâ, and reaching the palace of Sugriva, sent in Aṇgada to announce his coming; but the monkey-king, alarmed at the news that he seemed angry, hesitated to go forth to welcome him. Hanumân reminded of him of his promise to help Râma, still unfulfilled although autumn had arrived, and advised him to meet Lakshmaṇa with gentle apology, remembering all he owed to Râma's aid. Lakshmaṇa coming on through the palace to the inner apartments, Sugriva became still more alarmed, and sent Târâ to propitiate him, who softly prayed him to explain his angry entry. Lakshmaṇa reminded Târâ of Râma's grief, unthought of by her husband plunged in pleasures, and prayed her to counsel them as to what they should do. Târâ excused her husband, for the moment led astray by pleasure, but urged that he had already summoned his armies; and she prayed Lakshmaṇa to enter the room where Sugriva sat amid his wives: "For the good to behold the wives of others in a friendly spirit cannot cause unrighteousness."

Greeting Sugriva, Lakshmaṇa sternly and harshly reproached him for his ingratitude, declaring that unless he redeemed his promise he should follow Vâli on the road of death; but Târâ interfered, excusing Sugriva's carelessness, and praying Lakshmaṇa not to yield to anger like an inferior man, but to show gentleness and friendship. Then Lakshmaṇa, ever generous though hasty, conquered his anger, and Sugriva prayed forgiveness, promising to set forth with Râma. On this Lakshmaṇa, in turn, asked forgiveness for his harsh words, and they shortly set forth together to Râma, at the head of a vast army.

Then Sugriva sent out bands of monkeys to the four quarters with orders to search for Sîtâ, the band that went southwards being commanded by Aṇgada, and including Hanumân, Nila, and other famous monkeys. For one month they were to search and then to return, and great were the rewards promised to the happy finders of Sîtâ. [§§xxix—xlii.]

Seeing the confidence reposed in Hanumân by the king, and knowing who Hanumân was and his powers, Râmachandra called him, and, giving him a ring bearing his own name, He bade him give the ring to Sîtâ, who would thus feel assured of his good faith. Forth went the four bands of searchers, leaping and boasting, but, when the month was over, three of them returned crest-fallen, for nowhere in the East, the West, the North, was Sìtâ to be found.

Meanwhile Aṇgada and his band were also searching fruitlessly the South, and, wearied and despondent, knew not what more to do. They had reached the Southern ocean ; no further could they search. The month expired, and they dropped helplessly on the ground, not daring to turn back, their task unfulfilled. Hanumân strove to win them to return, but Aṇgada sat down to starve himself to death, unwilling to face Sugriva after failing in his task. His followers surrounded him to share his fate, and, as they lay fainting there, a vulture, Sampâti, elder brother of Jaṭâyu, came out of a neighbouring cave, rejoicing that food had thus come to him. Aṇgada, hearing him, faintly remarked to Hanumân that they were dying for Râma's sake, as Jaṭâyu had done, and the vulture, thus apprised of his brother's death, eagerly enquired what had befallen him, explaining that Jaṭâyu was his younger brother, and that he had himself lost the use of his wings in once shielding Jaṭâyu from the burning sun. Aṇgada told the story of the search, and prayed Sampâti to help them to discover Sîtâ; and he told them that he had seen a fair woman being carried away by Râvaṇa, and that probably she was Sîtâ. Now Râvaṇa lived in Lankâ, a city on an island eight hundred miles across the southern sea. The vulture sight, developed by the food on which vultures feed, ranged over a little more than eight hundred miles, and using this, he could see Râvaṇa and Sîtâ in far-away Lankâ. [§§xliv—lviii.]

Truly here was news of Sîtâ, but who among the monkey host could cross this heaving ocean of eight hundred miles? One said he could bound eighty miles, and another one hundred and sixty, and so on and on. Only Hanumân was silent, the mighty son of the Wind-God. Jâmbavân, an ancient bear, called on him, reminding him that he was the son of Vâyu, and could leap, as could his father, coursing through the air. And Hanumân, thus summoned, changed his form to a huge size, fit for soaring in the sky and for cleaving the ocean, and then, concentrating his mind, "he mentally went to Lankâ." [§§. lxiv-lxvii.]

This phrase, as to doing an action mentally, often occurs in the *Râmâyaṇa* and other sacred writings, and in this mental doing is the secret of success. Man's weakness lies less in his incapacity of execution than in his incapacity of thought. Strong, clear, exact thinking accomplishes the greater part of any action; its execution in the physical world is secondary. Hanumân, mighty in action, begins his exploits by clearly picturing them in his mind, and then he proceeds to the triumphant carrying of them out.

Ascending a mountain, and saluting the sun, Hanumân bounded forth on his tremendous flight. Coursing through the clouds, upborne by his father the wind, dashing aside the waves as he sometimes dipped into the ocean, he rushed on his road, meeting with strange adventures and winning his way through all, till Lankâ rose on the horizon, and Hanumân, contracting himself to his native form, alighted on her shore. [Sundarakâṇḍam §. 1.]

There he remained till night-fall, puzzling over some plan by which he might seek for Sîtâ, unperceived by the Râkshasas, for if they found him too soon, his mission would fail of success. When the sun had set, he reduced himself to the proportions of a cat, and, in that humble guise, slipped into the guarded city. But at the very gate he was met by a foe, a huge deformed female, the city itself in elemental form, who, detecting him, strove to stop him, but he struck her down, and she, yielding, bade him go on his way. [§§. ii, iii.]

Then be began his search through Lankâ, and saw many a lovely woman, and many a happy home and joyous scene, but nowhere saw he Sîtâ, and his heart grew sad and heavy. Through palace after palace he sought, into the innermost recesses of Râvaṇa's splendid home, till he came where Râvaṇa himself lay sleeping, surrounded by his wives, and, seeing one damsel passing fair, for a moment Hanumân thought he had found the beauteous object of his search; and, overcome with joy, he "struck his arms with his hands, kissed his tail, frolicked, sang, darted towards the pillars, shot up to the top of them, jumped down to the earth, shewing every sign of glee, exhibiting his monkey nature." [§§. iv.-x.]

But very quickly his loftier nature asserted itself, and he knew that this fair girl could not be the chaste Sîtâ, Râma's spouse, and again he set forth on his search. But nowhere was Sîtâ to be seen, and at length he began to despair. But saluting Râma and the Gods, he again concentrated his mind, and mentally entered the Ashoka wood and pictured a meeting with Sîtâ. Passing from thought to action, he sprang into the wood, and searched it in every direction, finally climbing into a tree whence he could see far and wide. Then he beheld therein a palace, and—O joy of joys! there was Sîtâ, the long-sought, pale, with soiled garment and jewel-less, Her head bowed with grief, Her sad eyes full of tears. Ah! this indeed was Sîtâ, Sîtâ as he might expect to find Her. Not in the golden palace, not in the hall of feasting, not amid wanton women; but here, sad and drooping, alone save for Her terrible guard—thus indeed might he look to find Râma's spotless wife. [§§. xi.-xv.]

Then Hanumân, praising Râmachandra and Sîtâ in his heart, watched Sîtâ with delight, wondering at her strange and fearful guard of Râkshasîs, some with fierce animal faces, and others variously deformed, hairy and distorted, with twisted and misshapen limbs. They were drinking wine and devouring raw flesh, and their bodies were sprinkled with blood from their hideous feast. Presently, through the night, came Râvaṇa, followed by a crowd of his fair wives, and at the sight of him Hanumân climbed higher in his tree, that the great Râkshasa might not see him. And Sîtâ, the helpless, trembled as he came, as a hind approached by a tiger. Tenderly Râvaṇa addressed her, bidding her not to fear, and sueing humbly for her love: "Having created thee, the artist of the Gods, creator of celestial beauties, ceased from his work. O Maithilî! become my bride, the foremost queen of these my lovely wives. All the jewels I have gathered from the three worlds and all my kingdom I give to thee. Râma has resigned all hope of rejoining thee. Come, be satisfied, enjoy!" So pleaded he, for he dared not take her by force, since a curse had been pronounced on him of death if he bent an unwilling woman to his pleasure.

Weak with weeping, worn and faint, Sîtâ's words came low but firm: "Take back thy mind from me, and place it on thine own wives. Devoted to one husband, I will never commit sin." Turning away Her face from his burning eyes, She gently pleaded to him for morality and his own safety. "With wealth or riches thou canst not tempt me. As the rays of the sun belong to him, so am I Râghava's alone. May good befall thee, O Râvaṇa, take me back to Râma. Make friends with Râma, He is kind and gracious. There is no safety for thee if Râghava, the lord of men, be angry. Thou wilt be destroyed." So spoke Sîtâ, unflinching, alone and at the mercy of the mighty chief. [§§. xvi.-xxi.]

Then Râvaṇa burst into fierce threats, and finally gave her two months' grace, after which She should be forced to yield, or thereafter should be slain; but Sîtâ answered boldly, defying all his power, and Râvaṇa, calling the Râkshasîs, again commanded them to bend Her to his will by fair means or foul, and thus left Her in anger, foiled yet once more. For truly is it written of Her, that in all Her sorrow, "Her heart did not lose its loftiness," and that "Sîtâ, of dark-blue eyes, was protected by virtue of Her own character." [§. xvii.] For ten months She had dwelt in Lankâ, surrounded by every terror, yet was Her heart strong, Her courage unbroken. For gentleness does not mean weakness, nor sweetness lack of strength. She was brave as She was tender, loyal as She was loving.

When Râvaṇa had disappeared, the Râkshasîs thronged round Sîtâ, urging Her to yield to his suit, and threatening Her with death if She persisted in Her refusal. But Sîtâ remained firm alike against bribes and threats; "Eat me up if you will; I will never follow your words. Poor, or deprived of kingdom, He who is my husband is my guru. I am ever devoted to Him." Threatening Her with weapons and with clenched fists, menacing her with being torn in pieces, "like a fawn surrounded by wolves," She shrank back from them, but still through Her tears She sobbed: "Eat me up if you will; I shall never follow your words." She walked slowly and feebly, pursued by the Râkshasîs till She reached the tree wherein sat Hanumân, watching the scene, and there She sank on the ground and piteously bewailed Her fate. But in that host of enemies, one friend appeared, Trijatâ, old and wise, and she bade the Râkshasîs stand back, as she had dreamed a terrible dream. She had seen Râma and Lakshmaṇa in a celestial chariot, and Sîtâ clothed in purest white met Râma, "like unto light joined to the sun." Various others things she saw, foretelling the triumph of the brothers, whereas she had seen Râvaṇa falling headless to earth, and plunged into foul dirt, and she had seen his brothers and sons—all save Bibhîshana—going southwards, to the quarter of Yama, king of death. And she advised the Rakshasîs to make friends with their captive, whose triumph was surely near at hand. [§§ xxii—xxix.]

Meanwhile Hanumân, perched in the tree, was wondering how he could communicate with Sîtâ without arousing the attention of the Râkshasîs. At last he decided to softly tell Râma's story in Samskrit with Sîtâ's capture by Râvaṇa, and concluded by remarking that the monkeys were searching for Her, and that he had found Her. Hearing the voice, and much surprised, Sîtâ looked upwards to the tree, and there saw a big monkey, seated on a bough. This sight by no means comforted Her, but rather added to Her fears, which were not allayed when the monkey dropped down in front of Her. He was, however, a gentle and polite monkey, and addressed Her with joined palms, asking who She was and what Her grief, and was She Râma's Queen? and Sîtâ, rejoiced when She heard Her husband's name, quickly told Her name and related what had befallen Her. Then Hanumân told Her of Her husband's welfare, and Her heart was glad; but sudden suspicion struck Her, as Hanumân drew a little nearer, that he was Râvaṇa disguised as monkey, and She shrank away in new terror, bidding the monkey speak Râma's praises, if he indeed was friend and not hidden foe. Then Hanumân sang His praises, and presently described His person, and finally he gave Her Râma's signet-ring, thus vanquishing Her doubts. [§§ xxx—xxxvi.]

Then Sîtâ prayed him to urge Râma to hasten His coming, as ten months had passed, and when a year was complete She would be slain. Thereon Hanumân prayed Her to mount on his back. and he would carry Her to Râma, but She refused, partly from fear, but more from womanly modesty, unwilling to touch the person of another than Râma. Further, it was for Her husband to deliver

Her, and not for any other. Then Hanumân praised Her highly, declaring Her decision to be worthy of Râma's spotless wife, and begged Her to give him some token to bear to Râma, that He might know Her to be really found. So She told him a story to repeat to Râma, of an incident that happened when They were alone together, and She gave him also a splendid gem, which She had hidden away in Her cloth, and which Râmachandra would recognise as Hers. And Hanumân, having comforted Her with the promise of Her husband's speedy coming, went his way. [§§ xxxvii—xl.]

But he had no mind to depart without provoking a struggle with the Râkshasas, and after turning matters over in his mind—strange mingling of divine intelligence and monkey mischief—he began to destroy the grove attached to the palace of Râvaṇa's queens, the fair Ashoka wood, all save the spot where Sitâ lay, and then, magnifying his body to huge proportions, stood quietly, awaiting attack. Swiftly was the news carried to Râvaṇa that a huge monkey had talked with Sita, and had ravaged his grove of pleasure, and Râvaṇa, furious, sent out his guards to punish the bold intruder. And Hanumân, roaring aloud, proclaimed his name, and shouted victory to Râma, and then met his assailants and soon routed them utterly.

As the remnant fled before him, Hanumân, taking a prodigious bound, alighted on the top of the great temple of Lankâ, and his shouts of "Victory to Râma! Victory to Lakshmaṇa! Victory to Sugriva! Hanumân, son of the Wind-God, is Râma's slave!" rang through the fair city and carried terror into all hearts. As the guards of the temple sallied out, he wrenched up a heavy pillar and whirled it in the air, firing the temple and slaying the guards, and still his roars of defiance filled the air. One chief after another went forth against him, and still the mocking monkey shouted and slew, bounding hither and thither, now high in air, now perched on some pinnacle or roof, dealing blows which might have seemed but rough wild play, were it not that they carried death. "No monkey is this," quoth Râvaṇa in fury, "some being is he, born of Yoga to annoy us." And he sent five of his best generals against him, but they shared the fate of their predecessors. Then prince Aksha went, fiercest of warriors, and after a terrific duel, fell dying to earth. And at last Indrajit, the mighty son of Râvaṇa went forth and engaged Hanumân, and fiercely raged the combat, neither able to subdue the other. Then Indrajit, resorting to meditation, found that Hanumân could be bound but could not be slain, so he shot at him a Brahma weapon, that, on striking, bound the foe in bonds he could not break. And Hanumân, lying helpless, thought to himself that it would be a good thing if the Râkshasas carried him bound to Râvaṇa. He had wanted to see him; perhaps this was the divine way of granting him his wish. "Very great benefit," said he to himself, shaking with inward laughter," "shall I derive from my conversation with him." To keep up the game, he began to moan piteously, as the Râkshasas bound him with ropes of bark and cotton, rejoicing all the time at their ignorance; for the binding force of a Brahma weapon vanishes when other bonds are added, and he knew he could burst the ropes in pieces when he would. "Alas!" said Indrajit to himself, "these Râkshasas have rendered useless my great deed. They know not the action of mantras. And on the Brahma weapon being baffled, no other weapon can do aught. Truly we are now in a perilous strait." For Indrajit was wise as well as brave, and was a master of celestial weapons.

As Hanumân was carried bound into Râvaṇa's presence, looking sad and piteous outside, but merry at heart, the great Râkshasa bade his counsellors enquire who and what he was. "An envoy am I," quoth Hanumân the wily. "Why did he ravage the grove and slay the guards?" was the natural question, for truly these were strange deeds for a peaceful envoy. Said Hanumân meekly; "The peerless grove I ravaged in order to see the famous lord of the Râkshasas;" as for the combats, the Râkshasas attacked him, and he must needs defend himself. He needed to see the king on Râghava's business; let the king listen.

Then Hanumân spoke seriously and wisely, praying Râvaṇa to set Sîtâ free, describing Râma's power, whom none might overcome in battle; but his words so angered Râvaṇa, that he furiously ordered his servants to close the speaker's lips in death. But his brother Bibhîshana quickly interposed, reminding Râvaṇa that an envoy must not be slain; this was a universal law, respected by all. If an envoy committed crimes, he might be punished, but he must not be put to death. Even in his fierce anger, Râvaṇa bowed to the law of the sacredness of an envoy's life, and praising his brother, he harshly and scornfully declared that as a monkey was very fond of his tail, it was fitting punishment that this one's tail should be set on fire. Then the Râkshasas bound cotton steeped in oil round Hanumân's tail, and set fire to it, and then began to carry him round Lankâ, crying, "This is a spy." News of this was carried to Sîtâ, whose tender heart was pierced with the idea of the suffering of Her friend, and She approached a fire and prayed the Lord of Fire, by Her faithfulness to Râma, to become cool to Hanumân. The flame leaped up in answer, and Vâyu also breathed cold air on his son, and Hanumân wondered why he felt no pain and why his tail was cool though flaming. Then, weary of the farce, he suddenly burst his bonds, and slew the guards, and stood thinking what he should do. Surely as the sacrificial fire had been lighted, it was but right to pour offerings into it; and thus thinking, Hanumân began a wondrous dance. He sprang from house to house, from fort to fort, from palace to palace, and set them on fire with his burning tail; bounding through the air like a flashing meteor, he burned all which he touched, till fires roared beneath him echoing his roars of mischief and of victory, and all the city was one flaming mass, her beauty withered, her palaces burning ruins. Then Hanumân quenched his tail in the ocean, and felt his mind at rest. [§§xli—liv.]

But suddenly a horrible fear seized him: was Sîtâ burned? In his wild mischief he had forgotten Sîtâ. Had She fallen a prey to the flames? But he heard some celestial beings say that Jânakî was unhurt, and paying Her a hasty visit to assure himself of Her safety with his own eyes, he then set himself to cross the ocean once again. Back he went to the northern shore, shouting with delight, and eagerly was he welcomed by his waiting friends, who encircled him, leaping, shouting, in ecstacy of gladness. And Hanumân told his story, and when the uproar of delight that succeeded it had been partially calmed, the monkeys set forth on their return journey. [§§lv.—lx.]

After a characteristic scene of mischief and riot on the way [§§lxi.—lxiii.], the monkeys arrived at the camp of Sugriva, and began to relate their story. But Râmachandra longed to hear of Sîtâ, Hanumân was made spokesman, and described all he had seen in the Ashoka grove, delivering Sîtâ's message and placing Her jewel in Her husband's hands. Touched was Râma to the quick, seeing the gem bereft of the fair face which had ever shone beneath it, and folding Hanumân in His arms, He embraced him tenderly, fit reward for his loving service. [§§lxiv—lxviii, and Yuddha-kâṇḍam §. i.]

Then, the first joy over, the difficulties of the task before them occupied their thoughts. How cross the occan? how reach the far-off Lankâ? Râma, ever energetic, urged Sugriva to set forth at once, and speedily the huge army was on its way, and ere long reached the southern ocean and saw its tumbling billows stretching far away. [§§ii—v.]

Meanwhile in Lankâ preparations were being made for war; confident were the Râkshasas in the might of their chief, and little they recked of the stories of Râma's prowess. Only Bibhîshana was anxious, for he was pure and pious, of Râkshasa form but righteous mind, and he pleaded with Râvaṇa to send Sîtâ home to Râma. But he stood alone amid a host of foes, and none of his arguments prevailed; then Râvaṇa rebuked him harshly before all the council, and Bibhîshana thereupon renounced him, and took his way to Râmachandra, abandoning Râvaṇa to his fate. [§§vi—xvi.]

Arrived at the camp of Sugriva, Bibhîshana met at first with no friendly welcome. Sugriva hastily and naturally condemned him as a spy, but after much discussion Hanumân spoke in his favour, and counselled his acceptation, while Râmachandra was willing to receive him: if a friend he should be protected, while even if he were an enemy, there was no crime in giving him shelter. Quickly answered Sugriva that one who forsook his brother in time of danger could never be trusted: but Râma said placidly that the Râkshasa could not injure Him, and that in any case His rule was to protect any friend or foe who sought His protection. Even if

Râvaṇa come to Him for shelter, He would declare to him, "have no fear." So Bibhîshaṇa was given shelter, and Râma promised to seat him on the throne of Lankâ, there and then sprinkling him as king of the Râkṣhasas. Thereupon they asked his advice as to the crossing of the ocean, and Bibhîshaṇa advised that Râma should beseech the aid of the Ocean himself; so for three nights Râmachandra lay on the sea-shore, praying to the Ocean, but he would not show himself. Then Râma, angry, declared that He would dry up the ocean with His fiery arrows, and began to loose them: and the wild creatures of the ocean were terrified, and roared and leapt, and presently the Ocean himself arose and bade Râma cease. And he told Râma that the monkey Nala, the son of Vishvakarmâ, might build a bridge across his waves, and he would hold it up, and the sea should be as firm land for the crossing of the monkey host.

Then the monkeys gathered trees and crags, and toppled them into the ocean, and so for five days they laboured, until the bridge reached the further shore. And Hanumâna took Râma on his back and Angada took Lakshmaṇa, and some monkeys swam beside the bridge, and others bounded along it, springing high in air; and thus, in tumult and with uproar, amid shoutings and roarings,

Râmachandra crossed the ocean, and stood on the land whereon Sîtâ had been awaiting His coming for ten long months of pain. [§§xvii.—xxiii.]

CHAPTER VII.

STRUGGLE.

Arrived on the island of Lankâ, Râma quickly marshalled his forces, and then bade Sugriva set free Shuka, a spy of Râvaṇa, whom the monkeys had captured. And Shuka fled swiftly to Râvaṇa and told him that Râma had reached his shores with hosts consisting of thousands of bears and monkeys, so that he must either give Sîtâ back, or do battle with her husband. Angrily answered Râvaṇa that neither for Gods nor Dânavas nor aught else would he surrender Sîtâ, for had he not fought with Indra, Varuṇa and Yama, and who was this Râma that He should stand before him in battle? [§§ xxiii. xxiv.]

Then Râvaṇa bade Shuka go once more and spy out the enemy, taking Sâraṇa with him, and, disguising themselves as monkeys, they found the hosts too numerous to reckon. Discovered by Bibhîshaṇa and taken by him to Râmachandra, the kindly prince bade him loose them, and let them go and tell all they had seen; whereupon, returning to Râvaṇa, they urged him to seek for peace: "Dispute is hopeless. Do thou render back Maithilî to Dasaratha's son." But once again came the stern answer, "Sîtâ will I not part with for fear of any."

Ascending his palace roof Râvaṇa surveyed the mighty hosts of his foes, "boundless and irresistible," and Shuka and Sâraṇa described the chiefs: among them Râmachandra Himself, "the hero of dark-blue hue, with eyes like lotuses," and Lakshmaṇa of the colour "of pure gold, broad-breasted, having dark curled hair." But with all he saw, his courage remained unshaken, and ever he repeated: "Sîtâ will I not part with for fear of any." [§§ xxv.-xxx.]

But with his foes menacing him, Râvaṇa was not forgetful of his thwarted passion, and sending for Vidyajjibha, who was "gifted with the powers of illusion," he bade him take an illusory head of Râma and a great bow and follow him to Sîtâ. Then he shouted to Her as he came near that Râma was dead, had fallen in battle, for his own army had fallen on that of Râma and had destroyed it, and Prahasta had found Râma sleeping and had smitten off his head, and many leaders had been slain and Lakshmaṇa had fled: "Bring Viddyajjibha," he cried, "who has brought Râghava's head!" And he came and threw the head down before Sîtâ with a mighty bow.

Ah! sad then indeed was Sitâ as never before, seeing that noble head, blood-stained and dust begrimed, and She fell swooning. And then, recovering, She clasped the dear head close and wailed over it in pathetic accents, pitifully lamenting Her beloved. "O Râvaṇa! speedily slay me upon Râma Do thou join my head to His and my body to His body." And as she wept, Râvaṇa was summoned hastily away, and lo! as he went, the head and bow vanished, and once more Sîtâ fainted away. Then a Râkshasî, Saramâ, who loved Her, came and tended Her; and when She had revived, she told Her that She had been deceived by an illusion, for Râvaṇa was then consulting with his counsellors how to meet and conquer the army he had pretended was destroyed. And thus she cheered her, till Sitâ's heart was again at peace. [§§ xxxi.—xxxiv.]

Some may suppose that this is a quite impossible story, and that no one could thus produce an illusory head, that could be seen and felt. But the European experimenters in hypnotism have shewn that such illusions can be very readily produced, and that people can be made to see and feel objects which have no physical existence. That this was such an object is shewn by its sudden vanishing on the departure of Râvaṇa, who held

Sîtâ under the illusion. Many of us have seen such illusions produced in modern days, and know by our own experiments that these old stories are no impossible inventions, but records of facts that can be still seen.

Meanwhile Ravaṇa was consulting with his ministers, and his maternal grandfather, Mâlyavân, argued forcibly for making peace with Râmachandra; but Râvaṇa indignantly repudiated the idea that Râma, a mere man, with a host of monkeys and bears at his back, could cope with himself, who had met the Gods in battle. "He before whom even the Gods cannot stay in the field, how can that Râvaṇa ever come by fear? Better that I should be riven in twain—but bend I never will." Thereupon he arranged the defence of the city, himself guarding its northern gate, and as the opposing army also marshalled its forces, Râma chose for his own post the one in face of his great foe.

On the morrow, as the chiefs stood on the mount of Suvela, surveying the city, Sugriva caught sight of Râvaṇa, and moved by a sudden impulse the monkey king flung himself on the gateway where Râvaṇa stood, and dashed off his crown; then the two grappled with each other fiercely, and for a long time they strove, neither gaining the advantage, until at length the stalwart and agile monkey tired out the Râkshasa, and bounded back again rejoicing to his friends.

Then Râmachandra bade Aṇgada take his message to Râvaṇa, bidding him either surrender Vaidehî or fight Her husband, and on the young prince entering and delivering his message, Râvaṇa gave angry orders that he should at once be slain. But when four Râkshasas seized him, with sudden bound he sprang on the roof of the palace, and the impetuosity of his leap made them slip off him and they fell to the ground, while he, stamping hard on the palace top, split it asunder, and them sprang high in air back to his own friends. Thereupon the monkeys rushed to the assault, pounding at the gates of Lankâ with crag and tree, and crushing the golden tracery, and soon the two opposing forces were in a death-grapple, and the roar of battle went up from every side. [§§xxxv.—xliii.]

Even the setting of the sun did not separate the combatants. Through the dark night they fought on unceasing, and prince Aṇgada won high distinction by pressing so hardly on Indrajit, that Râvaṇa's mighty son had recourse to his magic powers, and disappeared from before his youthful but gallant foe. Then, remaining invisible, Indrajit covered Râmachandra and Lakshmaṇa with a shower of arrows, flaming serpents that bit and bound them as they struck, until Râma dropped senseless to earth, and was soon followed by his younger brother; while their invisible foe, shouting with joy, proclaimed aloud his victory over the sons of Dasharatha, and after wounding Jâmbavân the king of bears, and Hanumân and Aṇgada and many another, Indrajit, believing that Râma and Lakshmaṇa were dead, re-entered the city of Lankâ amid the shouts of the rejoicing Râkshasas.

Ah! then indeed came the triumph of Râvaṇa, who bade the Râkshasîs take Sîtâ to the field of battle and let Her see with Her own eyes the dead body of Her best beloved. And they placed Sîtâ on Pushpaka, the wondrous car that Râvaṇa had wrested from Kubera, the God of riches, and drove to the field covered with the dead and dying; and there Sîtâ again beheld Him whom She had not seen since She sent Him from Her to hunt the golden deer, and there He was lying, pierced and senseless, His armour torn, His body thickly pierced with shafts. Piteously the tears broke forth from eyes well-nigh drained by weeping, and She bewailed Her husband, calling to memory all the prophesies and signs that foretold Her crowning with Her husband, and not the sad doom of widowhood. All were falsified, since Râma was no more. Saddest of all was queen Kaushalyâ's fate, she who was looking for her loved son's return. But Trijatâ, the wise, consoled Her, bidding Her note that the warriors were guarding the bodies, and were shewing neither fear nor anxiety; for, indeed, Bibhîshaṇa did not believe the brothers to be slain, and had bidden Sugriva guard them until they recovered consciousness. Comforted by Trijatâ's words, Sîtâ breathed softly, "May this be so," and then returned to Lankâ. [§§ xliv.-xlviii.]

Ere long, Râma recovered consciousness, and feebly looking round, saw His loved brother lying beside Him on the ground, and broke out into pathetic lament. "Of what use unto me the regaining of Sîtâ, or of life, when to-day I see my brother vanquished in fight, stretched on the field. Searching though the world, I might find a woman like Sitâ, but never a brother, a friend, a warrior like Lakshmaṇa. What shall I say to Kaushalyâ? What to Kaikeyî? What to our mother Sumitrâ, eager for the sight of her son? How shall I say to Shatrughna and to the illustrious Bharata, 'he went with me to the forest, but I return without him.' For me Lakshmaṇa lieth on the field of battle, like one deprived of life. O Lakshmaṇa, thou hast ever comforted me when I was unhappy, but to-day, having lost thy life, thou canst not console me in my sorrow. As thou didst follow me to the forest, so will I follow thee to the house of death." And He bade the army retire, since He would die beside His brother. Surely Râmachandra's loving heart was now riven in pieces; it had been pierced by Sîtâ's loss; it was broken by the slaying of his brother.

But listen! there is a sound of wind in the air, and flashing lightnings play; there is a beating of mighty wings, and through the storm like flame of fire, meteor-like rushing, comes Garuḍa, vehicle of Vishṇu, monarch of birds, enemy of the serpent-race. And as he comes, the magic serpent-arrows glide hissing away, wounds heal up at the touch of his body, and the brothers rise up, radiant and mighty, "with a double share of strength." "Who art thou?" asks Râma wondering, and the mighty bird, with eyes pleasure-gleaming, answers: "I am thy friend—thy life ranging outside thee, Garuḍa am I." And caressing Him tenderly he speaks again: "My friend Râghava, thou who lovest even thine enemies, give me leave to go. Be not curious as to our friendship. When success shall crown thee, then shalt thou understand our friendship. Slaying Râvaṇa thine enemy, thou shalt regain Sîtâ." For Garuḍa knew what Râma, flesh-prisoned, knew not, that this young warrior was Vishṇu, whom he bore so often on his back ranging through the realms of space. [§§ xlix. l.]

Now Râvaṇa, rejoicing over the death of his foes, hears roars of delight sounding forth where there should be shrill lament for the dead; and his heart is troubled within him. Swift messengers are sent to seek the reason of the unexpected mirth, and they return, pale and terror-stricken; Râma and Lakshmaṇa, bound by the death-noose of Indrajit's magic shafts, are free and are ranging the battle-field, like elephants that have burst their tether. Then Râvaṇa's face changed, and he felt his security was in peril, since his two enemies had escaped the magic bonds; and he bade Dhumrâksha, the mighty, go forth, and seek to slay Râma and his hosts.

Again the fight raged furiously, till Dhumrâksha and Hanumân met in deadly duel, and Hanumân, with a huge crag, struck his foe to earth; and then the Râkshasas rolled back on Lankâ, followed by the triumphant monkeys. Then Vajradanshtra, with mighty tusks, went forth where Aṇgada stood embattled, and they strove till the young prince conquered, and another leading Râkshasa lay headless on the ground. And Akampana sallied out, he who brought the news from Janasthâna, and met his death at the hands of Hanumân, struck down by an uprooted tree. Who next should go forth and face the death-storm? Râvaṇa cast doubtful eyes around the diminished circle of his generals, and they rested on the well-tried Prahaṣta, one of the chief leaders of his hosts. What says Prahasta? "I had declared myself before in favour of surrendering Sîtâ, seeing that the withholding of Her meant war. But ever have I been honoured by thee with gifts and regard and kind words. What good of thine is there for which I would not struggle? I care not for my life, not yet for wife nor sons. Behold! for thee I will offer up my life in the sacrificial fire of battle." So forth went the faithful soldier, ready to perish, and after gallant combat met his death at the hands of Nila, who crushed him with a huge crag, and once more the broken forces, sorely dispirited, rolled back on Lankâ. [§§ li.–lviii.]

Then said Râvaṇa that the foe who could slay Prahasta, who had destroyed the armies of Indra, was one that could no longer be treated with disregard. Himself would take the field—Râvaṇa the haughty, who had disdained to fight an army of monkeys and bears, headed by two men—he would go forth and destroy them, leaders and hosts alike.

Forth fared the Lord of Lankâ, and with him

Indrajit, and Nikambha, and other famous chiefs, and he shone in resplendent array flashing with jewels, radiant as the sun, so that Râma's eagle eyes were dazzled by his "exceeding glowing splendour." Waving back his forces, he bade them stand at ease, while alone he plunged into the hosts of his enemies, dealing destruction around him like Yama himself. And Sugriva fell senseless, and Hanumân faced the foe, and as he struck him Râvaṇa cried, "Well done, O monkey! thou art a worthy foe." And with a mighty blow, he left Hanumân powerless, and met Nila, who for awhile, while all the hosts wondered, held the mighty Râkshasa in check, yet fell at last, wounded well-nigh to death, yet not quite slain. Then Lakshmaṇa dashed forward and engaged him, and pressed him hard, while Râvaṇa wondered at his prowess, and both were sorely wounded, yet fought on, till Lakshmaṇa was pierced through the arm with a fiery arrow, and was seized by Râvaṇa; but he who had shaken Himavân and Meru could not move Sumitrâ's son, for in this crisis he remembered he was a portion of Vishṇu, and that knowledge made him strong as the Preserver of the world. While Râvaṇa strove to move him, Hanumân rushed against the Râkshasa chief and smote him with his clenched fist, so that he sank down senseless, and then he snatched up Lakshmaṇa and carried him out of the press. Then going to Râmachandra, who was rushing towards Râvaṇa, he prayed Him to mount on his back for the onslaught, and Râma rode on him as Vishṇu rides on Garuḍa. Then dashed together in deadly conflict Râma and Râvaṇa, and beneath Râma's terrible arrows, car steeds and charioteer fell riven in pieces. And on Râvaṇa's chest fell a shaft like a thunderbolt and he staggered and let fall his bow, while another lightning dart severed his jewelled tiara in twain. But Râma checked his hand, and listen! His grave clear accents ring out stern yet sweet: "High and glorious deeds hast thou performed, and my foremost heroes are lying slain by thee. Weary must thou be, and I will not therefore bring thee down to the gate of death. Go thou, worn-out as thou art, enter Lankâ and rest, thou and thy warriors. Afterwards, mounted on thy car, thou shalt behold my power." Was it but a dream that in Râma's eyes there shone a great compassion, the memory of Vishṇu for His Bhakta, who chose brief enmity that he might the sooner again seek His Feet? Was it for this that Râmachandra said so gently: "Go thou home and rest"? [§ lix.]

Humbled and discouraged, the lion-like Râkshasa in Lankâ recalled to memory the many curses brought on him by his evil deeds, but even though assailed by fear, resolved to make a last desperate struggle. He sent to awaken Kumbhakarṇa, his brother, a Râkshasa of vast strength, whose magic slumber lasted for many months at a time, and whose huge appetite, when roused, threatened the world with ruin. Vast mountains of food were heaped up ready to appease him on his awakening, deer and buffaloes and bears, and great piles of rice. Outstretched he lay asleep, huge as a great hill, with limbs extended, and his breath drove away, like a strong wind, all who approached his face. To awaken him they beat drums, and blew conches, and shouted and yelled; and they struck him heavy blows with crags and maces, but still he slept on calmly, the only quiet one in all that surging crowd. They bit his ears, they poured water on him, they thumped on kettle-drums, and yet he slept on. Only when a thousand elephants rushed against him, as they might have rushed against a mountain, did he at last awake, and got up yawning. Dumbly they pointed to the piles of food that rose around him, not daring to speak lest he should break out in fury, and Kumbhakarṇa fell upon the food and gorged his fill.

His appetite appeased, he began to wonder why

he had been aroused, and he asked the trembling onlookers why they had awakened him; was the king well, did some peril threaten him in which aid was needed. "One doth not awaken one like me for a light cause." Thereon they told him briefly what had happened in the siege of Lankâ, how what no God nor Daitya nor Dânava could do had been done by Râma, a mere man; Râvaṇa had been in danger of his life from him, and had by him been permitted to go free. At this Kumbhakarṇa furiously exclaimed that he would slay Râma and Lakshmaṇa and the monkey hosts, and a message arriving from Râvaṇa asking him to come to him, Kumbhakarṇa, shaking the earth with his tread, looking like a moving mountain, strode heavily to Lankâ.

Joyfully was he welcomed by his brother, who briefly recounted the dangers that surrounded Lankâ, the terrible slaughter of the Râkshasas, the apparently undiminished hordes of monkeys that swarmed around. Never before had he asked help, but now fear had sprung up in his heart. Kumbhakarṇa replied by blaming his brother for having brought this trouble on himself by an unrighteous act, thus arousing Râvaṇa's anger, who reminded him that he, as elder, was to be served, not reproved. Useless to blame the past; let help be given in the present. Then Kumbhakarṇa soothed him, promising to slay his foes, and bidding him cast away all sorrow, relying on his brother's matchless strength. And thereon he put on his golden armour and went forth, armed with huge weapons and a mighty dart, and, as he came, the monkeys fled in all directions, for who could face the shock of this man-mountain, eager for battle? [§§ lx.—lxv.]

But Aṇgada, undaunted, rallied his flying forces and they assailed Kumbhakarṇa on all sides, but again broke away, helpless against his giant strength. Again Aṇgada rallied them with burning words and keen reproaches, and they assailed the foe with renewed vigour, and Hanumân, facing Kumbhakarṇa, smote him with a huge crag which sorely hurt him, but his return blow pierced Hanumân's broad chest, so he staggered back, disabled for the moment. Then Aṇgada assailed him, and stunned him, but, quickly recovering, he stretched his assailant senseless on the ground. Sugriva next attacked him, and as Kumbhakarṇa whirled his dart to smite him, Hanumân caught the dart, and snapped it across his thigh. Then Kumbhakarṇa struck Sugriva senseless with a crag, and picking him up, strode away with him, hoping thus to disperse his enemies, deprived of their king.

But as he went through Lankâ, Sugriva awoke from his swoon, and, monkey-like, he clawed off his captor's nose and ears and tore his sides, and Kumbhakarṇa cast him off, as a man might throw off a stinging insect, and tried to crush him on the ground; but the lithe monkey sprang away with a tremendous bound, and regained his own army.

Enraged, Kumbhakarṇa returned to the field and began devouring the monkeys, till Lakshmaṇa faced him, covering him with arrows. Kumbhakarṇa was so struck with his courage that he bade him go, for not even Indra, mounted on his elephant and encircled by the celestials, had thus faced him in combat. And leaving Lakshmaṇa on one side, Kumbhakarṇa rushed on Râma, who with swift arrows deprived him of his weapons, but none of His shafts, though they pierced the gigantic body of His foe, were able to disable him or even to give him pain. But presently Râma with a keen weapon severed the mighty arm that whirled the mace, and arm and mace went hurtling through the air, and slew many a monkey as they fell. And a second shaft cut off the remaining arm, and two keen crescent disks shore off the ponderous legs, and only the huge trunk and head remained, with open mouth roaring tumultuously. But swiftly came the shining weapons, and the great head was severed from the trunk, and rolled to the ground like a falling avalanche, and the trunk itself fell, partly into the neighbouring ocean, and partly blocked the gate of Lankâ. So Kumbhakarṇa the mighty, the type of material unspiritual nature, passed away from earth, and with him the last hope of Râvaṇa. [§§ lxvi. lxvii.]

When Râvaṇa heard of his brother's destruction, heart-struck he swooned away, and recovering broke into wild lament. "O hero! O humbler of the enemy's pride! O mighty Kumbhakarṇa! Forsaking me, thou hast gone to Death's abode! I have nothing to do with empire. What shall I do with Sîtâ? Deprived of Kumbhakarṇa, I do not even care to live. If I do not slay in battle Râghava, the slayer of my brother, even death is too good for me, this life is useless. This very day will I go whither my younger brother has gone." Thus piteously Râvaṇa bewailed his brother, and fell on the ground lamenting. [§ lxviii.]

Then the princes that remained gathered round him, consoling him, and declared that they would face the foe once more and wrest victory from defeat. And forth they went, a gallant band, and charged upon the enemy. Again the battle raged, and many a heroic deed was done on each side, and Aṇgada and Hanumân performed prodigies of valour, and Mahodara and Narântaka and other Râkshasas were no whit behind. But one by one the Râkshasa leaders fell, while the chiefs of the opposing hosts still ranged the field.

Then Râvaṇa's mighty son, Atikâya, who had conquered the Gods and had oft routed the Dâṇavas, maddened by the loss of his father's noblest warriors, raged through the battle, till the heroic Lakshmaṇa faced him with stretched bow. "Go back!" cried Atikâya, "thou art but a boy: why would thou fight with one like death himself?" "Boy or old man," cried Lakshmaṇa, "death shalt thou meet in the combat;" and a fierce duel began. Well matched were the foes, skilled in the use of celestial weapons, discharged with magic formulæ, and evenly raged the contest and long it lasted. But at last the Wind God bade Lakshmaṇa—who wondered why his keen arrows fell blunted to the earth—use against his foe a Brâhma weapon, since to all others he was impervious. Then Lakshmaṇa set an arrow on a Brâhma weapon and loosed it at his enemy, and hissing it rushed forth; in vain Atikâya strove to turn it off, to sever it in twain; resistless it flew onwards, alive with flames, and struck the diademed head of Râvana's son and severed it from the body, and all for him was over. At his fall the Râkshasas fled, terror-stricken, and rushed to Lankâ wailing, filling the air with cries. [§§lxix—lxxi.]

Yet one was left of the mightiest, Indrajit, the conqueror of Indra, and as Râvaṇa, heart-broken, sat thinking of the ruin spread around him, his heroic son strove to cheer him: "Grieve not, O father! for Indrajit yet breathes." Then Indrajit sallied out, and on the battle-field ere engaging in combat offered sacrifice to the Fire with rice and flowers, and guarded his war-chariot and bow with mantras. Thereafter charging against the foe, he singled out the chiefs, and laid Sugriva and Aṇgada and many another senseless on the ground. And making himself invisible, he scattered arrows in all directions, and struck down Hanumân and Jâmbuvân and Nila, with other leading chiefs. Then spoke Râma to Lakshmaṇa, holding his soul in patience where help there was none: " This foe has obtained the Brâhma weapon, and rendering his body invisible is assailing us. How can we slay him who has hidden his body ? For to-day, my brother, bear this with me, and let him cover all sides with his shafts. Seeing us also fallen helpless, this enemy of immortals will go home." So spoke Râmachandra of indomitable patience, strong in defeat as in victory. And as he said, so it fell out. For as they ceased to fight and fell, Indrajit returned home rejoicing, and told his glad story to his father. [§§ lxxii—lxxiii.]

Then Hanumân and Bibhîshaṇa searched the field, to see what leaders were still breathing, and found Jâmbuvân, the wise, the king of bears, faint but yet living. And he bade Hanumân go with the speed of the wind to Himavân, and there, close to Kailâsa, he should find the mountain of medicines, where were four sovereign remedies which he should bring. And Hanumân rushed through the air as the wind rushes, and reached Himavân and saw Kailâsa and all the marvels of that famous spot, and the mount of medicines flaming in the midst, and Hanumân searched for the four sovereign remedies, and found them not, and, furious, tore the mountain from its base, and bore it through the air, as a whirlwind carries trees and stones in its outrush. And when he again reached Lankâ, the very fragrance of those herbs healed the monkey hosts, and the wounded sat up, and the slain arose, and all Indrajit's work was undone. And Hanumân took the mountain back to its place, and returned to Râmachandra, well content. [§§ lxxiv.]

That night an assault was made on Lankâ, and Râvaṇa sent the two sons of Kumbhakarṇa, Kumbha and Nikumbha, to repel the besiegers, but, after a furious combat, Kumbha was slain by

Sugriva—himself sorely injured—and Nikumbha met his death at the hands of Hanumân. Then Makarâksha, the son of Khara, went forth, but died, as had died his father in Daṇḍaka, by an arrow from Râmachandra's bow ; whereon Indrajit was sent out by Râvaṇa once more, and, again offering sacrifice, he vanished, and fought invisibly, while Râma and Lakshmaṇa strove to slay him by shooting in the direction whence his showers of shafts came forth. And Indrajit produced other illusions and made a figure of Sîtâ appear, while he, becoming visible, seized it by the hair, preparing to strike off its head. Beside himself with wrath, Hanumân cried to him to desist, but Indrajit with jeers struck off the figure's head, and the monkeys, believing it to be Sîtâ, fled away. [§§ lxxv—lxxxi]

Hanumân, however wild with rage, rallied the monkey-host once more and assailed the Râkshasa forces, until he drew off, saying that Sîtâ was dead and that further struggle was therefore useless. Going to Râmachandra, he delivered the news of Sîtâ's death, and Râghava dropped senseless, like a tree whose roots are severed. Lakshmaṇa in vain tried to restore him, and bitterly said that virtue was evidently useless, since such calamities befell a man so perfect : his very virtues had led him to misery. As Lakshmaṇa thus spoke, Bibhîshaṇa appeared, and on hearing the news said that it was most improbable, Râvaṇa having far other views for Sîtâ than death. The whole thing was a delusion manufactured by Indrajit. Now Indrajit had just gone to offer sacrifices, and if those sacrifices were completed he would be invisible. He must be interrupted ere they were finished, for it had been prophesied that thus he might be slain. Then Râma bade Lakshmaṇa go with Hanumân, and with Jâmbuvân, king of bears, and slay the Râkshasa so potent in illusions, and Lakshmaṇa set forth gladly, eager to serve his brother. The army thus led furiously assailed the hosts of Râkshasas encircling Indrajit's sacrifice, and pressed them so hard that at last Indrajit, in desperation, rose ere his sacrifice was completed and thus placed his head in the fatal noose of death. For Lakshmaṇa, mounted on the back of Hanumân, now met him in deadly duel, and long they fought and furiously, and neither would yield. Indrajit's car was shattered, and a second war-chariot used by him shared the same fate. Magic weapons were used on both sides, and baffled each other, till knowledge, as well as strength, was strained to the uttermost; at length, taking an Indra weapon, and bidding it slay the son of Râvaṇa if Râma were righteous and truthful, Lakshmaṇa with it struck off the head of

Indrajit, the conqueror of Gods, the shield of his mighty father, and as his body rolled on the ground headless, the stormy sky grew bright, and the earth became smiling with clear streams, and flowers filled the air, and all the celestials rejoiced, while the monkey and bear hosts roared and shouted round Lakshmaṇa, crying aloud the praises of Dasharatha's heroic son. [§§ lxxxii—xci.]

Heart-broken was Râvaṇa indeed when this worst of news reached him, and recovering from the dread shock a grim determination entered him to take a fell revenge: "By his power of illusion my beloved child, to deceive the woodrangers, slaying something showed it to them as Sîtâ. Now will I do that good office myself. Vaidehî will I slay, her who is devoted to that friend of Kshatriyas." So saying, Râvaṇa caught up a sword and rushed to the Ashoka grove, intent on slaying Sîtâ. But one of his courtiers, Suparshva, greatly daring, faced his king in his fury and persuaded him to stay his hand, and not soil his fame by that worst of acts, the slaying of a defenceless woman. Rather let him slay her husband, and then Maithilî would be his own. So Râvaṇa desisted, and went back gloomily to his house. [§§ xcii. xciii.]

While Râvaṇa sat mourning, his armies, still gallant, went forth yet once more, bidden by Râvaṇa to attack Râma only, whom if they failed to slay, he would himself destroy on the morrow. And this they strove to do, but instead of having to seek Râma, Râma seemed to meet them everywhere; thousands of Râmas seemed to be on the battle field, and yet He sometimes seemed to vanish, for His movements were so swift that the eye could not follow them. And Lankâ was filled with weeping as the Râkshasîs lamented their husbands, brothers, sons, and they recalled the prophecy that a woman should be born who should cause the ruin of the Râkshasas, and that, they wailed, was Sîtâ. [§§ xcii.-xcv.]

As Râvaṇa heard the piteous cries of the Râkshasîs, he grew wrathful, and bade them yoke his horses and bring his weapons, and then sallied forth himself to avenge his slaughtered relatives and chiefs, accompanied by the remnant of his warriors. Dire were the omens as he went forth, as all nature trembled at his anger and at the approaching combat of light and darkness. For now had come the final struggle for which Shrî Râma had been born; He was to face the Ruler of Evil.

Everywhere the monkey hosts gave way before his terrific ouslaught, but Sugriva in single combat slew Virupâksha and Mahodara, while Aṇgada conquered Mahâparshva, the three remaining generals who had mounted his war-chariot with Râvaṇa, as he sallied forth from Lankâ. Only stirred to greater wrath by his losses, Râvaṇa turned his arms against Râma Himself, and a tremendous duel ensued. Neither could succeed in injuring the other; each baffled the weapons of the other. Equal in knowledge and in skill they seemed, and all their magic weapons fell blunted from each. Lakshmaṇa meanwhile attacked the charioteer of Râvaṇa, slaying him, and Bibhîshaṇa killed his steeds, but Râvaṇa, undaunted, leapt to earth to attack his brother, and as Lakshmaṇa heroically threw himself in front of Bibhîshaṇa, the dart aimed at Bibhîshaṇa struck Lakshmaṇa. In vain did Râghava, as the dart hissed through the air, call out a benediction, intended to save His brother; the fury of the Râkshasa overbore the shield of love, and Lakshmaṇa fell senseless to earth. "No time for grief is this," cried Râma, as He saw His brother fall, and He pressed on Râvaṇa; but shortly, seeing that the monkeys could not pull out the dart from Lakshmaṇa's breast, He abandoned the conflict, and went to His brother's aid, while Râvaṇa poured a storm of arrows on His unguarded person. In a moment, He had pulled out the dart, and then turned again on His foe, and so furious was His attack that fear overcame Râvaṇa and he fled. Then Râma broke out into pitiful lament over Lakshmaṇa, fearing he was dead. "What have I to do with life? I have no more to do with fighting, seeing that Lakshmaṇa is wounded, lying in the field of battle. In land after land one meets with wives; in land after land one meets with friends; but country find I none where a brother can be met with. Ah my brother! Thou best of men! O master, foremost of heroes! Why, forsaking me, dost thou wander in other worlds? Why, brother, dost thou not answer me, who am lamenting. Get up! why dost thou lie down? Look on me with thine eyes." So He mourned, while Sushena strove to cheer Him, pointing to the signs which showed that Lakshmaṇa was not yet dead; sending Hanumân for a magic drug, Sushena crushed it and put it to the nose of Lakshmaṇa, and he revived and stood up. Then Râma clasped him warmly to His breast, rejoicing, and crying: "By good fortune, O hero, thou comest back from death. Without thee, life, victory, Sîtâ, are worthless."

But Lakshmaṇa, ever careful of his brother's honour, was ill-pleased that Râghava should be tending him while Râvaṇa was still unconquered, and prayed Him to make good His promise by destroying the Râkshasa. [§§ xcvi.-cii.]

Then Râmachandra turned again to seek Râvaṇa, who meanwhile had obtained another chariot, and, to make the combat more equal, Indra sent to Râghava his own car, driven by his charioteer Mâtali, with his mail, and arrows, and bow, and dart, and the two met in battle on their chariots. Râvaṇa shot shafts that turned into fiery serpents, and Râma met them with arrows that became birds like Garuḍa destroying them. But Râmachandra was hard pressed by His enemy, and the celestials trembled, while the ocean tossed wildly and the sun was dimmed, and Râvaṇa flung a dart like a thunder-bolt, that even Râghava's arrows could not destroy, but were burned by it as a flame burns up insects. Then the wrath of Râmachandra grew hot within Him, and He flung Indra's dart against that of Râvaṇa and broke it, and He showered arrows on him till he was bewildered and could not struggle with them, and then Râghava held His hand, seeing him helpless, and his charioteer drove him away from the field. But, recovering, Râvaṇa furiously rebuked his charioteer, who had made him look like a coward in face of the foe, he who was burning for battle, and bade him drive him back at once, ere his enemy had left the field. Meanwhile the great Agastya, who had come thither to see the combat, bade Râmachandra recite the Âdityahṛidaya, the great hymn to the sun, and He, obeying, concentrated His mind and bent all His forces to His task. Then the two chariots rushed the one against the other as thunder-clouds rush, and the crash of meeting was as the thunder-clap and the flaming weapons as lightning flashes, and the vultures gathered and the jackals howled, and stormwind whistled and the sky was black. All other combat ceased as they met, and monkeys and Râkshasas stood still to witness the dread encounter. The chariots whirled, each charioteer seeking an advantage, and arrows showered; one of Râvaṇa's heads was cut off by a shining arrow, but another at once took its place, and so many a time. But Râvaṇa fought on undaunted, and for seven days and nights that furious combat raged unceasing. At last, Râmachandra raised His mightiest weapon, created by Brahmâ for Indra, made of the essence of all objects, and strong as Death himself. Consecrating it with Vaidik mantras, Râghava launched it at His foe, and it struck him full on the chest and cleft it, and from his hands fell down his weapons, and he sank down on his chariot, and from his chariot rolled to earth; and thus the Lord of Darkness gave up his body, and the purpose of the Avatâra was fulfilled. And Râma, in answer to the prayer of Bibhîshaṇa spoke, the pregnant words: "With death our enmity hath terminated and our object hath been accomplished. He is as dear to me as to thee; perform his funeral rites." [§§ ciiii.-cxi.]

The funeral ceremonies being over and Bibhîshaṇa installed as King of Lankâ, Râmachandra bade Hanumân seek Sîtâ, and bring Him news of her. Ah! joyous was then that faithful devotee as he sought again the sweet presence he had entered before in sore straits, and told Her the glad news of triumph, Râvaṇa was slain, Her safety was secured. Overcome by emotion, Sîtâ could not answer, but, recovering, She gave gentlest thanks to Hanumân, and sweetest praise. But when Hanumân begged permission to slay the Râkshasîs who had so tormented her, She mildly restrained him, saying that they were but servants, obeying their lord's command; further She told him that all suffering was by one's own acts, and that the inflictors of suffering were but instruments, and it was proper to show them compassion and not revenge. Then She sent Hanumân back to Shrî Râma, "I wish to see my lord, ever fond of those who are devoted to Him," and Hanumân returned to Râghava and repeated to Him Her words. [§§ cxii.—cxv.]

Hereupon Râma, silent, engaged in meditation, and afterwards, sighing deeply, He bade Bibhîshaṇa bring Sîtâ thither, robed in regal state. Joyfully the king bore the message, and when Sîtâ said in answer: "O Lord of Râkshasas, without bathing even I would see my husband," he answered gently: "It is fitting for thee to obey thy lord, Râma." Answering meekly, "So be it," Sîtâ bathed and robed Herself regally, with splendid garments and many gems, and, entering a palanquin, was borne into Her husband's presence. Coming out of deep meditation, Shrî Râma bade Bibhîshaṇa bring Her near to Him, and as Bibhîshaṇa was driving back the crowds encircling them, He checked him and bid him let them stay: "They are all my own men." Let Vaidehî, He proceeded, descend from the palanquin that all might see Their meeting.

Understanding from His grave accents that this was no merely joyous meeting of husband and wife long separated, Lakshmaṇa, Sugriva and Hanumân stood troubled, as the king led Sîtâ on foot to Râmachandra, and She came, in the royal robes that seemed to accentuate Her thin form and worn countenance, the tender face alight with love and joy, with eager longing hungry eyes fixed on the One that made Her sun on earth. "O gentle one!" spoke Râma with soft clearness: "destroying the enemies in battle, I have conquered thy foe, I have slain at one blow my dishonour and my enemy," And in a few brief sentences, He told the work that that been done. Wistfully Sîtâ gazed at Him, Her soft eyes filling with tears: was this Her husband's welcome ? what meant this formal greeting ? And as He saw Her near Him, so beloved, His heart was broken, for He knew—He had seen in His deep meditation—that should He yield to His deep love and take Her back after this year in Râvaṇa's evil house, Her innocence unproved, He would give bad example to all who regarded Him as ruler, and would seem to put His own passion above the good of His people, and the defence of purity of life. So, crushing back His own longing, He spoke again calmly and sternly : " The wrong inflicted by Râvaṇa has been punished : for thee I have laboured and have fought. But long hast thou lived in the house of another, taken on Râvaṇa's lap, gazed at by him with lustful eyes. Go thou wherever thou wilt. Settle where thou mayest please."

Conscious of stainless purity, of all She had endured for Her husband's sake, of Her long torment and unswerving faithfulness, what shall Sîtâ say ? The woman in Her weeps for a few moments ; then the hero-soul of Her asserts itself : " Why speak such harsh and unbecoming words, O warrior, as common man addressing common woman ? I am not what thou thinkest. Do thou believe me—I swear by my own character. O Lord, though my person was touched by another, it was not in my own powers, nor was it by any act of mine. My heart is under my control, and that is in thee: what could I do for my body, subject to another, I no more its mistress? Long have we lived together. If thou art not able to understand me, truly am I ruined for ever. Why didst thou not renounce me ere coming here, without risking thy life and burdening thy friends? Hadst thou so said by Hanumân, I had then and there abandoned my life. Thou does not honour my character enough, O thou that knowest characters. Thou art not sufficiently mindful of all my devotion and my blamelessness." Turning to Lakshmaṇa, She said steadily and firmly: "Make me a funeral pyre, O Saumitri: that is the only remedy for this disaster. Branded with an unfounded stigma, I do not care to keep my life."

Doubtfully Lakshmaṇa looked at his brother, but at His assenting gesture he prepared the pyre, and none dared speak to nor look at Râma, who stood as Death, and spake no word. Then Sîtâ, going round Her husband in mute farewell, with no word of pleading, no sign imploring mercy, spoke to the Fire: "O Fire, the witness of the people, do thou protect me, as my heart has never wandered from Râghava. As Râghava deems me vile, who am pure, do thou, the witness of the people, protect me on all sides." So speaking, with meek but majestic dignity, She entered the roaring flames, and as they rolled round Her She shone as gold, and then their gleaming hid Her, and wailings arose on every side as She vanished, and the high tongues of flame leaped up as though in triumph.

Then Râma again entered into meditation, and see, there appear around Him Brahmâ and Shiva, with the Gods of Water and of Death; where is then Vîṣhṇu, absent from this celestial company? "Why dost thou not know thyself, O Lord, the foremost of celestials, preserver of the worlds, the greatest of the wise, why dost thou not protect Sîtâ, entering into fire? Why does thou neglect Vaidehî, like an ordinary man?" Answered Râghava: "I know myself to be man—Râma, the son of Dasharatha. Let the Grandsire tell me who I am, and whence I have come." Then Brahmâ told Him that He was Nârâyaṇa, the bearer of the discus and the mace, the supreme Purusha, Viṣhṇu, the refuge of the saints, the supporter of the worlds; Sîtâ was Lakshmî; for Râvaṇa's destruction had He come down. His work was accomplished. Joyous, let Him re-ascend to heaven.

And as Brahmâ ended, Agni the God of fire, arose in the midst of the flames, and Sîtâ shone radiantly in his lap, as the fire arched itself round its Lord, like the hangings of a king's throne. "O Râma! here is thy Vaidehî, no sin hath touched Her. Shut up, with demons round Her, always Her mind remained in thee, and devoted to thee. Her heart is pure, and She is not spoiled by sin. Do thou therefore take back Maithilî."

Then Râma, having again meditated, answered: "The beautiful one lived in the inner apartment of Râvaṇa for a long time, so She needed this purification in the presence of all. If I should have taken back the daughter of Janaka without this, the people would deem Râma, the son of Dasharatha, to be lustful and ignorant of duty. I know full well that Maithilî, the daughter of king Janaka, hath her mind devoted to me and hath not given it to any other. As the ocean cannot overleap its bounds, so Râvaṇa could not approach Her, protected by Her own chastity. That vicious one could not touch Her even with his mind, for Maithilî was beyond his reach like the burning flame of fire. Her mind could not have been moved, even though She lived in the seraglio of Râvaṇa—She belongs to none else. Sîtâ is mine, as the rays belong to the sun. Maithilî, the daughter of Janaka, has been purified before the three worlds. Hence I am incapable of renouncing Her, as a righteous person cannot renounce his fame." Thus Râmachandra and Sîtâ were once more united. [§§ cxvi.—cxx.]

CHAPTER VIII.

TRIUMPH.

Ere the celestials went home, Maheshvara bade Shrî Râma see His father, Dasharatha, who had come with them to share in this glad hour, and Dasharatha, folding Him in his arms murmured that even heaven was not enjoyed by him in the absence of his son. And he went on to say: "The term of thine exile is over, thy promise hath been fulfilled. Placed in charge of thy kingdom do thou attain long life with thy brothers." And Râma prayed His father to remove his curse from Kaikeyî and her son, whom in anger he had renounced, and Dasharatha assenting, blessed Lakshmaṇa for his faithful service to Râma and Sitâ, and then he turned to Sîtâ: "It doth not behove thee, O Vaidehî, to be angry with Râma for renouncing thee, for, purifying thee, this was done by Him ever wishing thy good. What thou hast done, O daughter, to establish the purity of thy character, is hard to be performed. What thou hast done shall glorify all women."

As Dasharatha departed Indra spoke to Râma, bidding Him ask what He would, and Râmachandra asked that life might be restored to all the monkeys and bears who had perished in His quarrel, and that, wherever they went there fruits, roots, flowers and fresh water might abound. Indra granting the boon, the monkeys and bears arose, healed of their wounds, and the celestials went their ways, bidding Râma return to Ayodhya and there be crowned King. [§§ cxxi-cxxii.]

On the morrow Râma set forth for Ayodhya on the car Pushpaka, taken by Râvaṇa from his brother Kuvera, the God of riches, a splendid car, jewelled-decked and golden, hung with jingling bells, and adorned with paintings, huge as a mountain, with upper and lower rooms, bearing houses on its platform, and moving at will. Bidding Bibhîshaṇa distribute gifts to the soldiers who had fought so well, Râma ascended the car with Vaidehî and Lakshmaṇa, and was then followed at their own wish by Bibhîshaṇa, Sugriva and their hosts. As they sped through the air, Râma pointed out to Sitâ the battlefield, and the landing place where He and His army had rested after crossing the ocean, and Kishkindha, the city of Sugriva. There stopping at Sîtâ's wish, the wives of the leading monkeys were added to the company, and then again the car sped on, Râmachandra shewing Sîtâ the places where marked events had occurred on His search for Her and during Their years of exile. At last Ayodhya came in sight, and then Râma stopped the car, alighting at the hermitage of the ascetic Bharadvâja on the fifth day after leaving Lankâ. [§§cxxiii-cxxv.]

Hearing from Bharadvâja that all was well, Râma sent Hanumân to carry the news of His coming to Guha and to Bharata, bidding him notice whether Bharata were glad or sorry on hearing of it, since his mind might have changed after possessing the kingdom for so long; and if it were Bharata's wish, the kingdom should remain in his hand. Swiftly went the Wind-God's son, Hanumân, the bearer of glad tidings, rejoicing the heart of Guha, and then passing on to Bharata. He found him dwelling two miles out of Ayodhya in a hermitage, thin and worn, dressed as an ascetic, with the symbol of his absent brother, the sandals, ever before him, surrounded by his counsellors and soldiers, and protecting all. Hanumân, bowing before him, abruptly spoke out his news, and Bharata, weakened by long fasting, fell down in a swoon of joy. Then, recovering: "Art thou a man or a God who hast come here?" and he poured out joyous enquiries and longings to see his brother. Hanumân told him the whole story, Bharata eagerly drinking in his words, and when he heard that Râma was close at hand and could be seen on the morrow, the cry escaped his lips: "After a long time my desire hath been fulfilled."

Then began a joyous tumult as Bharata issued orders to prepare for the coming of the King, and armed men on horse-back and on foot gathered by thousands, and Kaushalyâ and Sumitrâ and the other wives of Dasharatha came from Ayodhya, and Bharata started forth, the sandals still with him; and they journeyed till they saw Pushpaka hanging in air, and shouts arose: "There is Râma! there is Râma!" Ah! glad was then the meeting of the long separated brothers, as Bharata, bowing at Râma's feet, was caught to his brother's breast, and each greeted each, and Sugriva was welcomed as "a fifth brother," and Râmachandra touched His mother's feet, and greeted Sumîtrâ and Kaikeyî. Then Bharata put the sandals again on his brother's feet: "This thy kingdom, which thou didst leave in my care, I return to thee. Blessed is my birth and accomplished my desire, since to-day I see thee as King in Ayodhya after thy return. Do thou examine thy wealth, treasury, palace and army. By thy favour I have increased all these tenfold." Thus the faithful Bharata fulfilled his trust, more joyful in surrendering a kingdom than is one who gains it. [§§cxxvi.—cxxix.]

Soon the glad procession started for Ayodhya, how different from the sad one that had left it fourteen years before, though many of the chief actors were the same. Robed royally, the brothers came, and Sîtâ and all the wives of the monkey chiefs were resplendent with gems; high over all Râma towered in His splendid beauty, rejoicing the hearts of all. And on the morrow, placing Râma and Sîtâ side by side on a jewelled throne, Vasiṣhṭha sprinkled Râmachandra as King; and the jewelled crown of His race was placed on His head, and the celestials sent garlands, and Gandharvas sang and Apsarâs danced, and the earth was rich with crops, and all rejoiced, because Râma, the son of Dasharatha, had come to His own, and was crowned as King in Ayodhya.

Among the gifts given by Râghava to His fair wife at His coronation was a splendid necklace of pearls, and Sîtâ, taking it off Her neck, glanced wistfully at Her husband and the monkeys. Smiling, Râma answered Her unspoken wish: "Give the necklace, O lovely and happy one, to him with whom thou art pleased." And Sîtâ graciously stretched out Her hand to Hanumân, giving the precious toy to the faithful one who had come to her in her lonely grief.

Then Râma bade Lakshmaṇa share with Him

the royal dignity, sitting beside Him as associate Ruler on the throne; but Lakshmaṇa would not, caring more to be simple attendant upon Râma than to wear joint crown with Him. So Bharata was raised to that high dignity, and for ten thousand years they ruled the land.

Such reign as that, the world had never known, for everywhere peace and plenty flourished, and the people's hearts were glad. There were no widows in the land, nor deaths of children—all lived to a green old age. Famine was not known, nor fever, nor drought, nor theft, nor murder; rain and sunshine came in due season and rich crops crowned the fertile soil. Poverty was not, nor anxiety, nor restless fear, nor gnawing pain. Heaven it seemed rather than earth, for Lakshmî, who is prosperity, sat as Sîtâ beside Râma, and all the land was glad.

Thus ends the *Râmâyaṇa*, as many think, "composed by Vâlmiki in the days of yore," for this kâṇḍam concludes with the blessings promised to all readers of the poem, as is the wont of ancient books. [§ cxxx.].

The kâṇḍam called the Uttarâ is not regarded by many as a portion of Vâlmiki's famous work. This may be due in the minds of some to its contents, to the outwardly gloomy ending of the story in the cases of Sîtâ and Lakshmaṇa, the blameless and beloved. But the Uttarâkâṇḍam is full of instruction, for it contains the explanation of the previous events, and illustrates the working of the law of karma, that law which is the expression of the divine nature which is the foundation of the worlds, the ancient, the universal law of causality, from which neither Gods nor men, neither loftiest Îshvara nor lowliest insect, can escape.

The great lesson of this kâṇḍam is the universality of karma. Nothing in the manifested universe is left outside its sway. Gods and men, Râkshasas and Asuras, all alike are shewn to be within this law—and indeed, how should it be otherwise, since it is the divine nature. In the great kosmic process, in the growth of universes and worlds, in their risings and fallings, linking kalpa with kalpa, everywhere the law is seen. All live and work within it, none can escape or transcend it. In order to teach this lesson, amid others, Râma and Sîtâ came into the world as ordinary man and woman, living the human life—Râma who was Vishṇu, Sîtâ who was Lakshmî, inseparable while the universe exists. Who should be strong enough to work it out, to bear all human pain, rather than plant a seed of evil to grow throughout the ages, who should be willing to carry it through, save They whose very nature is expressed in it, and who are most of all servants of the Law because that Law is Themselves?

Now when Râma was ruling in Ayodhya, Agastya and many other great ascetics came to congratulate Him on His victory over Râvaṇa, and especially over Indrajit, even greater than his mighty father. In answer to His questions, Agastya told Him the causes of his powers. Pulastya, son of Prajâpati, disturbed in his austerities by the playing and sporting of Apsarâs and maidens of human birth, declared that any who came too near to his retreat should conceive a child. A girl, who knew not of this, strayed within the forbidden limits, and her father prayed Pulastya to marry her, and she was accepted by the sage as his wife, and served him meekly while he practised his austerities. Blessed by him, she brought forth a noble son, who received the name of Vishravâ, and grew up studious and ascetic. He wedded Bharadvâja's daughter, and a son was born to him whom he named Vaishravaṇa, who grew up into a mighty ascetic. Offered a boon by Brahmâ, Vaishravaṇa asked that he might have the power of maintaining and protecting people, and Brahmâ made him the fourth Protector of creatures, the Lord of wealth, and gave him the car named Pushpaka. To him was given as dwelling the then deserted city of Lankâ, built by Vishvakarma, the architect of the Gods. [Uttarâkâṇḍam, §§ i-iii.]

Now the daughter of Sumâli, a great Râkshasa, Kaikasî by name, being desirous of children, interrupted Vishravâ while performing the Agnihotra: he granted her children, but declared that only one of them, the youngest, should be righteous-souled; the others should be Râkshasas, she having disturbed the sacrifice. Of her were born Dashânana, the ten-faced, Kumbhakarṇa, Shurpanakhâ and the righteous Bibhîshaṇa. One day Vaishravaṇa was passing, and Kaikasî pointed him out to Dashânana as his brother, and bade him struggle to become as great as he was. Thereupon he and his two brothers betook themselves to asceticism, and Dashânana offered one by one nine of his ten heads as sacrifice; when he was about to strike off the tenth, Brahmâ appeared and offered him a boon. He asked for immortality, and on that being denied as impossible, he asked that he might be incapable of being slain by birds, serpents, Gods, Yakshas, Daityas, Dânavas and Râkshasas, disdaining danger from any others. This boon was granted, and he was further granted the power of taking any form he desired, while his sacrificed heads were restored to him. Bibhîshaṇa, offered a boon, asked that he might remain fast fixed in righteousness, and this was granted to him, with the immortality he had not asked for. Kumbhakarṇa was also offered a boon, but Sarasvatî took possession of his vocal organs, and made him say that he wished to sleep for a good many years; he too had his request granted, and slept marvellously, as we have seen. [§§ ix. x.]

Although Lankâ had been empty when Vaishravaṇa took possession of it, it had formerly been inhabited by Râkshasas, and Dashânana, instigated by his grandfather Sumâli, asked Vaishravaṇa to give it to him, and the generous lord of riches gave it to him, and went to Kailâsha. Then he wedded Mandodarî, the daughter of Maya, and of her was born Meghanâda, later known as Indrajit. Dashânana, having gained his boon of invulnerability against all he feared might compass his death, threw off the righteousness by which he had gained it and began to ravage the world. His elder brother Vaishravaṇa sent him a message, praying him to desist, but he slew the envoy, and set forth to attack his brother in Kailâsha. There he slaughtered the Yakshas, the followers of the lord of wealth, overcame his brother in single combat, and took from him his famous car, Pushpaka. As he was leaving Kailâsha in Pushpaka, the car suddenly stopped, and, as he wondered, Nandi, a servant of Shankara, appeared, and bade him go aside, for Shankara was sporting on the mountain. Inflated with pride, he said jeeringly, "Who is Shankara?" and came close to the mount. Seeing Nandi in a monkey-form, he derided him, and Nandi told him that in the future monkeys would destroy his race, and then, as Dashânana seized the mountain to drag it from its base, Mahâdeva playfully pressed it down with one toe, and prisoned his arms, and he lay there roaring, till he submitted to the blue-throated Hara, who thereupon let him go, giving him the name of Râvaṇa, the roaring, on account of the yells he had uttered. [§§xi.—xvi.]

Undeterred by this check, Râvaṇa continued to ravage the earth, and coming to Himavân, he saw an ascetic maiden of rare beauty, and though told by her that she was dedicated to Vishṇu, he seized her with evil intent; but she, wrenching herself away, lighted a funeral pyre and burned herself thereon, declaring to him that she would return to earth, unborn of woman, to bring about his destruction. This happened in the Kṛita

Yuga, and in the Treta Yuga she was born as Sîtâ from the furrow made by Janaka. [§xvii.]

Then Râvaṇa went on with his conquests, and forced all the kings of the earth to fight with him, or declare themselves defeated. And most submitted, but Anaraṇya, of the race of Ikshvâku, king of Ayodhya, fought, but finally fell under his death-blow from Râvaṇa, and, dying, said: "There shall spring in the line of the mighty Ikshvâku one named Râma, son unto Dasharatha, who shall deprive thee of life." Thus by his own evil deeds, Râvaṇa sowed for his own reaping the seed of death. [§§xviii.—xix.]

As Râvaṇa went on his way, he met Nârada, the sage, who counselled him to leave men alone, who were already sufficiently harassed by many evils, and seek to conquer Yama, the conqueror of all. The idea pleased Râvaṇa, and he started for the nether regions, slaying all the hosts of Yama that opposed him, until Yama himself came forth on his car, whereon in front stood Death, and the Rod of Time flamed beside him. At the sight all Râvaṇa's followers fled and left the Râkshasa chief alone, but undaunted he faced Time that conquers all. And for seven nights and days they fought, until at last Yama lifted his Rod to slay Râvaṇa. Then Brahmâ appeared, and bade Yama stay his hand, for He had bestowed on Râvaṇa a boon of safety and he must not falsify His words. For the Rod of Time was created by Himself to have power to slay any, and if it fell on Râvaṇa falsehood must result; for either it would slay him according to its nature, and then the promise to him would be falsified; or else it would not slay him, and then the word that gave it power would be falsified. "Therefore do thou keep thy uplifted weapon off Lankâ's lord. If thou hast any care for these worlds, do thou establish my truth." Then Yama held his hand, and, to put an end to the fight, vanished from the field; and Râvaṇa, deeming him vanquished, returned from Yama's realm. Next he fought against the Daityas for a year, and then concluded peace with them, and went on to attack Varuṇa. He was away, but his sons gave Râvaṇa battle and were slain. Still eager for battle, he went on, and came to the dwelling of Bali, guarded by a mighty figure, who bade him enter and fight Bali if he would. And Râvaṇa entered and saw Bali, who laughed, and pulling Râvaṇa like a child down on his knee, asked him what he wanted. Râvaṇa arrogantly offered to free him of the bonds placed on him by Vishṇu, but Bali laughed again, and bade him bring to him a flaming discus that lay on the floor. And Râvaṇa grasped it but could not move it, and on a second attempt fell down covered with blood. Then Bali told him that it was only a ear-ring of one of his forefathers, Hiranyakashipu, who was slain by Vishṇu as Narasinha—leaving him to imagine how he would face the One who conquered the Daitya whose ear-ring he could not lift. It was this Vishṇu whom he had seen at the door, Hari, Nârâyaṇa, the protector of the worlds. Then Râvaṇa rushed out, intent on fighting, but Hari, who for Brahmâ's sake, would not slay him, had vanished, and he went safely on his way. And many another adventure had he, that you may read at leisure, and one especially that rose up against him towards the end, to the helping of Sîtâ. He met a beautiful damsel and sought to possess her, and the damsel prayed him to spare her, as she was given to his brother's son; Râvaṇa, despite her pleading, took possession of her, and was cursed by Vaishravaṇa's son, who declared that he should fall dead if he ever again outraged an unwilling woman. [§§ xx.—xxxi.]

When Râvana went forth to battle with the Gods, he took with him Meghanâda his son, and great was the fight that raged between the Râkshasas thus led, and the hosts of the celestials. The tide of battle had turned against the Râkshasas, when Meghanâda rallied them, and, making darkness by his illusionary power, he crushed the celestials and enabled the Daitya chief Puloma to steal away Indra's son. Then Indra himself sallied out to fight and attacked Râvana, but was himself assailed by Meghanâda and turned aside to fight him. Then Meghanâda rendered himself invisible, and when Indra was exhausted, he bound him by magic illusion and carried him away prisoner to Lankâ. Thither came the celestials, headed by Brahmâ, to obtain the release of their king, and Brahmâ, bestowing on Meghanâda the name of Indrajit, asked what he would accept in exchange for Indra. Asking immortality and being refused, Indrajit prayed that whenever he offered sacrifice to the fire, ere engaging in combat, a chariot and horses might arise, and that he might be immortal while on that chariot, and let him meet with destruction whenever he began to fight without finishing his offerings to the fire. Thus he also sowed the seed of his own death, just as Indra, in his defeat and capture, had expiated a former crime committed against Ahâlya, the wife of Gautama. [§§ xxxii.—xxxv.]

Such were some of the causes which worked out in the story we have been studying. And now the remaining threads must be gathered up.

One evening, when Sîtâ came in to Râma, after the evening religious ceremonies were over, Râma asked Her what wish She had that He could satisfy, and She expressed a strong desire to go and visit the Ṛishis who were living on the banks of Gangâ. Râmachandra promised to arrange for Her to go on the morrow, and thus, leaving Her, joined His friends, who were sitting engaged in conversation. Presently Râma asked what was said of His brothers, of His wife, of Kaikeyî, in the towns and provinces. Vadra replied that many good things were said, and the people talked much about the destruction of Râvaṇa. Something in Vadra's manner aroused the keen observation of Râmachandra, and He bade him repeat anything, good or bad, that was said of Him, that He might amend anything that gave offence. Then Vadra answered that he would repeat the unpleasant things frequently dwelt on by people wherever they met together. They praised the wonderful deeds of Râma in bridging the ocean and slaying Râvaṇa, but they blamed Him for taking Sîtâ back after she had been with Râvaṇa. She had sat in Râvaṇa's lap, was kept by him guarded by Râkshasîs. They also then should permit bad conduct in their wives, since subjects should follow the footsteps of their King. Deeply grieved, Râghava asked of one after another if this were so, and they all sadly answered that the subjects were thus speaking of their monarch.

Then Râma dismissed the courtiers and sent for His brothers, whom embracing, with his eyes full of tears, "You are my all, you are my life," He bade them be seated. He then told them of the scandals current, and of the conclusions dangerous to public morality drawn from His own conduct regarding Sîtâ. He reminded them of His hesitancy in Lankâ, of the ordeal by fire and the approved innocence of Sitâ. In His own heart He knew her pure and chaste. But honour was dearer than happiness or life, and He must part with His wife. Let Lakshmaṇa take her to Vâlmiki, whither she wished to go, but let Her remain there. With a quick gesture of anguish He checked the protest rising to Lakshmaṇa's lips: "Do not say anything—do not ask me aught. Take Sîtâ away." Thus Râmachandra made the great renunciation of His life. [§§ lii—lv.]

Much has this action of Râma been challenged and criticised, and many have blamed Him for "sacrificing His wife to the malice of slanderers." How deep was His love for His wife had been shown in His struggles to defend and save Her. But He was King as well as husband, and His duty to His people came first and was Hers as well as His. King and Queen were They, and a nation's morality hinged on the example They set. What greater homage to virtue was possible than that They should live apart, if Their living together brought any slur on honour, encouraged any breach of female purity? Thus judged Râmachandra, and thus judged also Sîtâ, who was as Himself. She was sacrificed by Him but assented to the joint sacrifice, bitter for Shrî Râma as for Her. Listen to Her words to Lakshmaṇa, when he has falteringly explained his charge, to leave Her with Vâlmiki: there are a few words of natural shock and grief, and then: "Say to the pious king: 'Thou knowest, O Râghava, that Sîtâ is pure, ever devoted to thee and engaged in thy well-being. She knows full well that thou hast renounced her from fear of evil fame. It is her duty to put a stop to thy ill name and censure of thee, for thou art her excellent refuge.'" But when Lakshmaṇa had gone, human nature had its way, and Sîtâ sank down wailing. [§§ lvi.—lviii.]

The sons of the Ṛiṣhis, hearing the crying of Sîtâ, called Vâlmiki to Her aid, and he quickly came to Her, consoling Her with gentle words and bidding Her look on the hermitage as Her home. He took her to the female ascetics, who were living there as his disciples, and bade them tend Her with reverence and affection; there she dwelt, and in due course gave birth to two boys, named by Vâlmiki, Kusha and Lava, who grew up into noble youths within the circle of the ascetics. [§§ lix. and lxxix.]

Lakshmaṇa, returning sad at heart from his painful mission, unburdened his grief to the faithful Sumantra, and Sumantra told him that long ago Durvâsa had told king Dasharatha that Râma would renounce His wife and His brothers, but that the king had charged him to keep the matter secret. It seemed that the king visited Durvâsa and asked as to the future of his sons, and the Sage told him that during a battle between the Suras and Asuras, the latter had sought shelter with the wife of Bhṛigu. She protected them, and Vishṇu, being angry, cut off her head with His disc. He was thereupon condemned by Bhṛigu to take birth among men, and to be separated from His wife for many years. Vishṇu, for the sake of mankind, declared that He would slay Râvaṇa and then be subject to the curse. He had been born, said Durvâsa, as Râma, and would, after a reign of eleven thousand years, instal in Ayodhya His two sons by Sîtâ. Lakshmaṇa, greatly cheered, returned to Ayodhya, and, finding Râmachandra plunged in grief, urged Him to arouse Himself and do His duty as King, else were His abandonment of Sîtâ for His people's good in vain. [§§ lxx-lxxii.]

Shortly after this Shatrughna was installed as king of Madhu, then tyrannised over by an Asura named Lavana, and he set forth with an army to fight for his throne. On his way, having sent his army on in front, he stayed with Vâlmiki, and it was while he was there that Sîtâ gave birth to Her sons. Seven days further he journeyed, and then arrived near the city of Madhu, and was warned by the ascetics that Lavana could only he slain if he were without a death-dealing dart, given by Shiva to his father, and by his father bestowed on himself. While he was wielding this dart none could overcome him, and with it he reduced his enemies to ashes. On the following morning Lavana went out to collect food, and was intercepted by Shatrughna as he returned to his city. Challenged to fight, he desired to be allowed to fetch his weapon, but Shatrughna insisted on his fighting then and there. They fought and Shatrughna fell, but recovering ere Lavana had entered the city, he once again assailed him, and shot him with a celestial arrow, made by Vishṇu. Thereafter he settled in the city of Madhu, and ruled the land well, until, twelve years having passed, he longed to see once more Râma, his elder brother. [§§ lxxiii–lxxxiii.]

Travelling to Ayodhya, Shatrughna after seven days reached the hermitage of Vâlmiki, and was warmly welcomed by the Sage. After the evening meal, some music was performed, songs relating the actions of Râmachandra, and Shatrughna was overwhelmed with delight, but from shyness did not ask any question of the ascetic. Reaching Ayodhya the next day, He prayed Râma to let him remain with Him, but Râma bade him return to his duty at the end of a week, and Shatrughna sorrowfully obeyed. [§ lxxxiv.]

When some time had passed, Râmachandra determined on offering a horse-sacrifice, and to that in due course Vâlmiki came, together with many ascetics. Among the disciples of Vâlmiki were two youths of princely presence but ascetic garb, and he bade them sing the *Râmâyaṇa*, as he had taught it to them, his great poem of the life of Shrî Râmachandra, but not to care for wealth. They might sing it anywhere, and if the king should invite them, let them sing it fearlessly to Him. And Kusha and Lava went forth and began to sing, and Râmachandra heard them, and wishing to here the whole, He invited a great assembly and bade the boys chant the poem. When they had finished twenty sections, and everyone was delighted, and some said to their neighbours that the boys were astonishingly like Râma, save for their ascetic dress, the King bade Lakshmaṇa give them eighteen thousand gold pieces. But the lads said they were dwellers in the forest, what should they do with gold? Astonished, the King asked as to the authorship of the poem, and the boys said it was composed by Vâlmiki, and that he might hear the whole if he liked to visit the Sage. [§§xcvi.-cvii.]

Many days were spent in listening to that story, the *Râmâyaṇa*, and at last Râmachandra, hearing that the sweet and stately singers were the sons of Vaidehî, sent to tell Vâlmiki that if Sîtâ had lived a pure life in the forest, She should come, with His permission, and publicly make oath of Her purity. Vâlmiki having consented, a vast assembly gathered, and into the midst of it came Vâlmiki, followed by Sitâ, sweet and gracious as of old but worn and sad. In weighty words, setting his asceticism as pledge, Vâlmiki bore witness to Sîtâ's spotless purity and to the fact that the two noble boys, Kusha and Lava, were the sons of Râma Himself. Gently Râmachandra answered, that the word of the Ṛiṣhi was proof enough for Him: "Yet if Jânakî gives evidence of her own purity before the assembly, I shall be greatly satisfied." Then all the Devas came from the four quarters, headed by Brahmâ, to see the sweet Queen of heaven deign to make oath of Her purity before sinful men, and Râmachandra, seeing them, spoke again: "O foremost of Munis, the words of high-souled Ṛishis are free from sin, therefore on thy word only I shall consider Sîtâ to be of pure ways. Still all have come here, anxious to witness Sîtâ's trial. I shall therefore be greatly delighted if Jânakî gives before them testimony to her own pure character."

Then in the midst of listening Gods and men Sîtâ, the daughter of Janaka, spoke: Her soft clear accents rang through the vast assembly, sad with an infinite pity for Her slanderers, strong with a firm determination to stay no more here below. "I have never thought of any other person in my mind but Râma; by the strength of this virtue let the Goddess Vasundharâ give me room. I have always with my mind, body and words prayed for Râma's well-being: by virtue hereof, let the Goddess Vasundharâ give me room."

Then the ground split apart, and out of the cleft the Goddess of the Earth arose, seated on a splendid throne, and stretching out her arms to Sîtâ, she drew Her to her side and placed Her on the throne. And the celestials showered blossoms on Her, crying," Oh! well hast thou done, O Sîtâ!" And the jewelled flower-covered throne sank down into the earth, and Sîtâ, the earth-born, disappeared whence She came. [§§ cviii.—cx.]

Râmachandra sat speechless as She vanished, and then fast coursing tears rolled down His cheeks. She had left Him in the moment of re-union, and He knew that never again should the fair form of Sîtâ gladden His eyes on earth. "O Goddess, bring me back my Sitâ!" He cried at last; "I am beside myself for her; do thou therefore bring back Sitâ!" But Sitâ had gone where earth's voices could not reach Her, to

Where beyond these voices, there is peace.

And Brahmâ spoke: "O Râma! thou shouldst not grieve. Do thou once more remember thy birth from Vishṇu. By nature Sîtâ is pure and chaste, and ever dependent on thee. Thou shalt again meet her in heaven." Then Râma entered His palace, and spent the night mourning for Sîtâ.

Thereafter Râma ruled His kingdom sad at heart, refusing to marry again, and having in His palace a golden image of His vanished wife, which took Her place whenever He offered sacrifice. [§ cxi.]

And now the time was drawing near for His passing away from earth, and He began to arrange the future of His house. He established the sons of Bharata and Lakshmaṇa in neighbouring kingdoms, and as He was making these arrangements Kâla, Tîme, came to Him in the guise of an ascetic, and desired to speak with Him alone, and further prayed that any who interrupted them should be slain. And thus Râmachandra ordered, placing Lakshmaṇa on guard. Then Kâla told Him that He was Vishṇu, and that the period fixed for His stay on earth was over. He could remain longer or return home as He would. And Râma smiling said that He was thinking of this when Kâla came, and that He should now repair to His own place.

Now as they were talking, Durvâsa arrived at the gate and demanded to see the King, and Lakshmaṇa prayed him to wait as Râma was engaged in business. But Durvâsa angrily declared that if Lakshmaṇa did not at once communicate his arrival unto Râma, he would curse him and his brothers and their posterity with all the kingdom. Then Lakshmaṇa thought to himself: "My own destruction is far more desirable than that of all," and went to Râmachandra and told Him, and He hospitably entertained the ascetic, but remembered sadly the promise given to Kâla. Then Lakshmaṇa went to his brother, reminding Him of His promise and bade Him keep His word, but the king summoned all His council and laid the matter before them. And Vasiṣhṭha told Him that He could not falsify His word, for a broken promise destroyed virtue and without virtue the worlds would perish. "Do thou protect the worlds by suffering separation from Lakshmaṇa, in the interests of the preservation of the three worlds." And all agreeing, Râmchandra said to His best beloved: "O Lakshmaṇa, it is not proper to act against morality: I do therefore renounce thee; for the pious hold that destruction and renunciation are the same." Then Lakshmaṇa, turning, went to the river Saraju that flowed by Ayodhya, and engaged in tapas, and therein passed out of the body, and hailed by the celestials as the fourth portion of Viṣhṇu, he entered into peace, gaining this recognition of his flawless devotion to Shrî Râma that he preceded Him in liberation, and went in front of Him whom he had ever followed, waiting to welcome Him home. [§§ cxii—cxix.]

Lakshmaṇa having departed, Râmachandra proposed to leave the kingdom to Bharata and follow him, but Bharata refused and prayed him to instal His two sons, Kusha and Lava, and let Shatrughna know that his brothers were departing.

Assenting, Râma divided the kingdom between His sons and sent for Shatrughna, while the citizens of Ayodhya determined on forsaking the world and following their loved King to the woods or to death. Then Shatrughna resolved to follow his brothers in death as in life, and crowning his two sons in his stead, repaired to Ayodhya. And behold! armies of monkeys and bears flock in, and Sugriva is there, having crowned Aṇgada in his place, and there also is Bibhîshaṇa, and there come Hanumân the faithful, and Jâmbhuvân. Sugriva may go with Râma, as he wishes, but Bibhîshaṇa and Hanumân are to remain on earth, so long as it shall endure, and Jâmbhuvân and his seven followers are to live till the end of the Kali Yuga. To the rest, monkeys and bears, celestial-born in earthly forms, He said, their work being over: " Do ye all come with me."

Forth they all set next morning, and Vasiṣhṭha duly performed the ceremonies necessary for going to the next world, and as Râmachandra leaves the city the Goddess Shrî Lakshmî, who had been born as Sîtâ, appears on His right hand, and the Goddess Vasundharâ on His left, and His brothers follow Him, and a vast concourse, all happy and serene, intent on following Him to death. And now He reaches Saraju, and Brahmâ appears, surrounded by hosts of Devas, and as He prepares to descend into the waters, Brahmâ sounds forth solemn welcome: "Come, O Viṣhṇu! Glory to Thee! Refuge of all creatures; beyond the reach of thought, and known of none save of Mâyâ, thy former spouse! Come, in whatever glorious form thou choosest!"

Then Râma shines out radiant in His form as Viṣhṇu, with His brothers, and all bow down in worship and there is a great peace. And beaming love around Him, as He bends gracious eyes on those who followed Him, as they thought, to death, He bade Brahmâ assign them life in happy regions: "They are worthy of my respect, for they are my devotees, and have renounced their persons for me." [§§ cxx.—cxxiii.]

Thus all entered into bliss, and thus it ever is. Those, who for love's sake abandon life when Râmachandra's face seems set towards death, find more abundant life, and enter into His joy.

PEACE TO ALL BEINGS.